The Carbon Boycott

The Carbon Boycott

A Path to Freedom from Fossil Fuels

SAMUEL C. AVERY

Toplight

Jefferson, North Carolina

Library of Congress Cataloguing-in-Publication Data

Names: Avery, Samuel, 1949– author.
Title: The carbon boycott : a path to freedom from fossil fuels / Samuel C. Avery.
Description: Jefferson, North Carolina : Toplight, 2020 |
Includes bibliographical references and index.
Identifiers: LCCN 2020041103 | ISBN 9781476682839 (paperback : acid free paper) ∞
ISBN 9781476641393 (ebook)
Subjects: LCSH: Fossil fuels—Environmental aspects. | Carbon dioxide
mitigation. | Renewable energy sources. | Climate change mitigation.
Classification: LCC TD887.F69 A94 2020 | DDC 363.738/746—dc23
LC record available at https://lccn.loc.gov/2020041103

British Library cataloguing data are available

ISBN (print) 978-1-4766-8283-9
ISBN (ebook) 978-1-4766-4139-3

Front cover images © 2020 Shutterstock

Printed in the United States of America

Toplight is an imprint of McFarland & Company, Inc., Publishers

*Box 611, Jefferson, North Carolina 28640
www.toplightbooks.com*

To my long-time friend and companion,
John Oliver Brittain, Jr.

Table of Contents

Introduction

They Only Sell What We Buy

This book is not about the horrors of climate change. It's about how to prevent them.

Over and over again people ask, "What can we do? We know what climate change is and why it's happening, but we're not politicians and we don't work for utility companies. We feel powerless. We'd like to stop using gasoline, but we can't create a whole new infrastructure on our way to work in the morning. So how can people like us slow down or stop the onward rush toward climate disaster?"

I wrote this book for these people.

I wrote it for you.

But I'm asking a lot from you. I'm asking you to change your life. I don't ask this lightly, but I'm afraid you are going to have to stop using coal, oil, and natural gas—and sooner than you might think. Ending reliance on these fuels will change everything, permanently: no more coal for your electricity, no more gasoline for your car, no more natural gas to heat your house. I'm asking you to boycott fossil fuel. Stop buying it. That's how to get rid of it.

Sounds extreme, doesn't it?

Yes, but here's why it's doable: we have around thirty years from 2020, which gives us until 2050—mid-century, or thereabout. We have time. We don't have to stop using fossil fuel tomorrow morning. Let's be realistic and give ourselves, say, 20 years, and then another 10 years of grace time—but no more. When it's time to change jobs, move to a new house, or buy a new car, that's the time to make the big changes. The little changes can happen along the way. Changing our lives is bound to cause disruption—maybe a lot of disruption—but disruption can be minimized by making changes when they occur naturally in our lives.

To make a long-term carbon boycott successful, you should begin to make the transition in community with other people you know. Do it with your friends. Form a group. Form a subgroup that focuses on creating and enforcing the boycott within an existing neighborhood association, church group, book club, environmental group, or social clique. You are going to need support from others who share your concerns about the impact of carbon use on climate. So seek out like-minded friends, neighbors, and family. Talk about looking for an electric car, saving up for solar, cooking a plant-based diet, or walking to work. Commit to making practical changes now and being alert to opportunities to implement more significant changes down the road. Then go bowling, start the book discussion, or have a beer. Make it fun; make it social. Make it part of what keeps you together as a group. This is the way the boycott will work. Change yourself; change your community; change your world.

As I write this book, events are occurring in the world and in my community that are a part the picture I am presenting. Wildfires burn across Australia and California, hurricanes spiral up the coast of North America, and thermometers climb to new heights throughout the world. Closer to home, my local environmental group *100% Renewable Energy Alliance of Louisville,* aka, *100% REAL,* engages with the Louisville Metro Council in an ongoing quest for 100 percent renewable energy as our local utility company proposes a fossil fuel pipeline through a legally protected nature preserve just south of town. These issues are as local as they are global and our sphere of influence is often strongest where we reside. I will insert periodic updates on *100% REAL* progress as events develop in the course of this writing, as well as occasional global climate updates. The climate crisis evolves as we speak, as we write, and as we read. I look out the window and it is there.

There's one key strategy around which the success of the carbon boycott is based—don't blame the need for it on anyone else. Don't blame it on the oil companies or the greedy politicians. They might well be to blame, but don't blame them. The boycott will work better if you don't. The boycott will work better if you refer to *us* instead of *them*. Note that *I, we, me,* and *us* are first-person pronouns. They initiate action. *We* are in a much better position to do what we want to see done than *they* are. If we concentrate on trying to stop external forces, we will butt heads with them and expend the greater portion of our energy trying to defeat them. And what would happen if we were to defeat them? What would it be like if we were to get the oil companies and the utilities to stop burning coal and gas? Would that be some sort of victory? How would we run our computers, drive our cars, and heat our homes? I'm not saying utilities and fossil fuel companies are not responsible for what is happening; I'm saying we should not burn ourselves out trying to force them to be accountable. We should accept our responsibility for carbon emissions because that is where we hold the greatest agency. That's where we can be most effective. It is we, after all, who create the market for what the utilities and the oil companies have to sell. *They only sell what we buy.*

We need to stop buying fossil fuel, over time, in community.

The carbon boycott is going to be a social movement. It must become a social movement if it is to be effective. Social movements typically depend on an enemy—some person or group of people— to organize against. Organizing against an enemy is the quickest and surest way to focus attention. But we can't rely on that technique in this case. We don't have a good enemy. We're complicit in the use of fossil fuels, so rather than pointing our finger at an imaginary other, let us instead create a social movement without using blame as a tactic. The carbon boycott may be more difficult to initiate this way, but more effective ultimately. Social movements that focus on enemies end up depending on the enemy for their focus. When the enemy is defeated, or dissipates, or no longer acts inimically, the movement no longer knows what to do. A movement that defines itself in terms of the enemy will have no self-identity when the enemy is gone. Climate change is about everyone acting in concert with the natural world. The concept sounds too big to be true, but it is truly as big as it sounds. It's the whole sky and the whole Earth beneath it.

The big picture view is necessary because climate change is the first truly global crisis that humanity has faced. All previous crises throughout human history have been local or, if national, or international in scale, between specific groups of people. Climate affects humanity as a whole. The climate crisis is created by all people everywhere and will affect all people everywhere. It must be confronted globally, not by people in separate nations. Across the world, people will see the climate changing and adapt their lives to the new reality. There is no one outside the circle. We are all culpable, to one extent or the other, of contributing to the problem and capable of implementing the solution. People in all nations must unite to create global institutions to monitor, legislate, and enforce a coordinated response. If some of us point the finger at others, the others will adopt a defensive stance and point the finger back at us. The dispute itself would then become the issue rather than the underlying problem and would absorb attention and creativity on both sides. Let us instead concentrate on taking steps to address what is happening to us—to all of us— in the real world.

I go back and forth on the urgency of climate change, I admit. I know the science is right. Scientists don't form opinions easily. They can't. As soon as a scientist publishes a paper stating something he or she thinks is true, a swarm of colleagues tries to disprove it. Careers are made by presenting counterevidence and knocking down hare-brained concepts and newfangled theories. Very few new scientific "facts" emerge from the wreckage. A consensus is never complete; a few hard-nosed researchers always disagree with whatever truth seems to be trying to reveal itself. This is a good thing; opposition to what we want to believe helps sculpt the new reality. It keeps us from believing only what we want to believe. Objections to Copernicus's heliocentric theory of the solar system took over a hundred years to die down, and there are still those who object to Einstein's theory of relativity. Critics are a healthy addition to the scientific community, but the consensus is now clear: global warming is accepted by the vast majority of scientists. Current evidence of the impacts of climate change is precisely what science has predicted it would be. So I believe that, yes, to avoid the worst effects of climate change, we have about thirty years to completely rid ourselves of fossil fuel combustion.

But while living daily life, my conviction fluctuates. I see cars and trucks roaring down the highway. I hear air conditioners humming down the block and lawnmowers roaring on neighbors' lawns. I see smokestacks pouring black soot into the air. I hear politicians talking about jobs in the oil and gas industry. In my own house, the furnace and the refrigerator click on and off. It all seems so normal, but as new mega-mansions are built on the outskirts of town, a series of questions invariably runs through my head. Who will live in them? How long will they be able to live there? Am I out of step with a society that considers large scale development a sign of progress?

When skeptics abound, it's easy to begin to wonder: am I crazy? Is my understanding of the impact of climate change based on some sort of fad? Have I just found an "issue" to complain about? Will we ultimately just muddle through and move on to argue about another existential threat looming on the horizon? Not according to the abundant available data on how human activity affects the climate. Let's look through that window next.

1

The Physical Facts

It's very clear. Since we started burning carbon fuels:

- The atmosphere has 48 percent more carbon dioxide (2020).
- The average temperature has risen by 1.0° centigrade (1.8°F).
- Ocean acidity has increased by 25 percent.
- Half of the arctic sea ice has melted.
- Sea level has risen 13–20 centimeters (5–8 inches).
- There are five times as many people inhabiting the planet.
- June 2019 was the hottest month ever recorded in human history, until
- July 2019 was the hottest month ever recorded in human history.
- On July 25, 2019, the temperature in Paris, France, was 109° F; 5° F degrees above the all-time high.

These are the hard numbers. They are not opinions.

The physical basis for life on Earth has changed.

Note on Sources

Sources for factual statements in *The Carbon Boycott* are easily accessible online. Atmospheric CO_2 levels can be checked daily at *www.co2.earth/daily-co2*. Temperature records are available from the National Oceanic and Atmospheric Administration: *www.noaa.gov*. Most of the climate data quoted is from the United Nations Intergovernmental Panel on Climate Change: *www.ipcc.ch*. Other incidental information is accessible online through information provided in the text. The pellet mill in Northhampton, NC, for instance (*www.envivabiomass.com*), can be reached online by entering "pellet mill Northhampton NC."

The change in atmospheric chemistry is not a matter of local air pollution. Every cubic centimeter of the entire planetary atmosphere now has nearly half again as much CO_2. This is a permanent change, everywhere. The concentration of CO_2 in 1880 was 280 parts per million. A year ago it was 410 ppm. Today (June 6, 2020) it is 417.20 ppm.

This raises temperatures everywhere. The rise in temperatures is not only on hot summer days. Nights are warmer. Winters are warmer. Polar regions are warmer. Global weather patterns are changing everywhere. This is pleasant at times. But warmer temperatures mean more energy in the atmosphere. And more energy in the atmosphere means more storms, more wind, more rainfall in some areas, and more drought in others. There is more rain or snow in single weather events. Some areas maintain average annual precipitation while experiencing more rainfall *and* more drought at different times of the same year. Instead of an inch of rain thirty times a year, there might be three inches of rain ten times a year. Ironically, higher temperatures can also mean more snowfall in some areas. Thus far "global warming" seems to be revealing itself most visibly in more intense tornadoes, droughts, wildfires, floods, and hurricanes.

The change in oceanic chemistry is also planetwide. When CO_2 from the atmosphere dissolves in ocean water it forms carbolic acid, H_2CO_3, and spreads throughout the entire oceanic system. There is nowhere else for it to go. Acidity levels affect nearly all chemical reactions and biological processes. Coral and shellfish are particularly vulnerable because acid dissolves calcium, the primary element in seashells.

The area and thickness of arctic sea ice have decreased annually, especially in the last 20 years. The entire icecap is likely to disappear completely twenty to thirty years in the future. But because arctic ice is floating over an ocean rather than covering a continent, its meltwater will not cause sea levels to rise. Floating ice displaces the same volume of water as the water into which it melts. The worst effects of melting sea ice are the loss of the white reflective surface provided by ice and the increased exposure of the dark, heat-absorbing surface of ocean water. Less solar heat is reflected and more is absorbed, further warming the planet.

Sea level rise is caused by ice melting on land surfaces, particularly in Greenland and Antarctica (and, to a lesser extent, on mountain glaciers). Its effect will be felt in coastal areas, particularly at river deltas, where higher sea levels combined with storm surges, increased precipitation, and glacial melt will damage large areas of agricultural production and urban development. Sea level rise to date has been marginal but measurable. Its impact will become severe in the latter part of this century and the beginning of the next, as massive chunks of ice slide off Greenland and Antarctica and float on the ocean surface.

Today there is a fifth as much land for each of us as there was in 1880 when we started making measurable differences in atmospheric CO_2 levels. But each of us living an average American lifestyle, including our cars, houses, hamburgers, thermostats, strip malls and their accompanying parking lots, takes up more land now, not less. Something has to give.

It is very clear.

The *physical basis* of life on Earth—air, water, sunlight, and soil—has changed and is changing at an increasingly rapid rate. As the planet grows warmer, life itself—plants, animals, and people—will attempt to adapt, one way or another. Plants will live on in a modified form, and some animals, including humans, might adapt and survive, too. Maybe. But organized human life—*civilization*—will never be the same. We will not exist as we do now.

At this moment in time, it is also clear that without carbon fuels most people would die within a few years. Coal, oil, and natural gas are necessary for civilization, on a daily, personal, perennial, and global basis in first-world countries:

- The car sits waiting in the driveway.
- Power lines stretch overhead.
- The furnace kicks on and the refrigerator hums in the kitchen.
- Electric lights bring day to deep winter nights.
- Metal pipes burrow through basement walls.
- We're just sitting here with the television on.
- We are fed, connected, warm, and entertained.

This is what life is like in the average home in the United States.

Oil tankers skim the ocean surface. Fracking wells penetrate the bedrock. Pipelines pulse with methane, ethane, tar sands, and octane. Trucks and trains roar across the continent. Aircraft fill the sky. Diesel tractors plow the cornfields as cattle trample in feedlot mud. Natural gas is converted into fertilizer, into fuel to dry grain, into freezer fuel, and into the packaging of the products we buy. This is how we fuel our lifestyles.

We drive to a supermarket chain for meat, which we find on aisle five, well-lit, and sanitarily packaged, next to the dairy case. This is the way it is. This is the way it has been for a long time. There are seven days in a week and twenty-four hours in a day. Gravity pulls downward. This is how we live. Why question it?

It's very clear.

We rely on all of it. Our economy is based on people working to supply what we need. People build the roads, dig the ditches, lay the pipes, and search the hills for signs of coal and oil. People drive the trucks, assemble the furnaces and freezers, and work all day in the sun to harvest corn and wheat. We pay them because we need what they make. Needs shape our ways of doing and our ways of thinking. People must have food, shelter, and clothing. Once our needs are met, we can think about other things. It's hard to think straight when you are cold and hungry.

The structure of our economy wasn't designed as a whole. Nobody figured out how we would gather food and warm our houses. These things just happened. The pieces fell into place. The invisible hand showed us what to do, and we do it. Nobody thought up the big picture and put the pieces together. There never was a big picture. There did not have to be. But to address the global crisis of climate change we must step back and consider things as a whole and as we do so a big picture emerges.

That big picture comes not from what we think or plan. It is not what we want or choose for ourselves. It is what is *actually happening*, not what should happen.

There is a strong relation—a near causal connection—between the physical facts of climate change and how we define our needs as planetary citizens. We are causing a vast, existential disruption of the physical basis of life on Earth because we want things in excess of our needs. That's the big picture. It is bigger than we are. This sort of crisis has never happened before. It is happening now.

The big picture is not a plan. It is not intentional. It just is.

Why can't we see this? Why aren't we doing something about it? Why are we still driving cars, air conditioning offices, and checking the fridge for a snack? Adaptation to the new physical reality depends on how we understand our needs. So why don't we examine our needs? Why don't we look at what we are doing?

Because some correlations aren't so clear even in the face of the evidence.

Take the impact of human behavior on climate, for instance. The connection can be a hard sell because the climate is not a physical object. It is *average weather*. There is no point in time when, and no point in space where, you can see average weather. Climate is everywhere but nowhere in particular. It's a very real thing, but you can't point at it. You can't hold it in your hand. You can't show it to someone you are talking to. It's as easy to disregard or ignore as empty space. If you want to see it, you have to allow yourself to see it and many people chose not to. If you don't want to see it, you can look and not see it.

In some circles, the association of climate *change* with human behavior is met with skepticism and rebuttal. The rationale goes something like this, it *seems* we are getting more rain, more high winds, more fires, droughts, blizzards, heat waves, and tornadoes. But we have always had blizzards, heat waves, and tornadoes. There's nothing new here, except the frequency and intensity of weather events, or the *perceived* frequency and intensity. According to this line of thought, our awareness of climate change may be due to more satellite imagery and internet media. We know more now about severe weather in distant places, places beyond where we live. We hear more about fires and hurricanes. That may be what makes it *seem* like the climate is changing, but calm winds and clear days don't make the news.

To understand what climate change is, we need to look at data showing a *change in average weather*. But how do you define average weather? What parameters do you set? Are you trying to make a point when you select a particular location and a particular variable to study? Even for a single point on the Earth's surface, you can always find new deviations from the average, or you can find old averages by combining droughts and floods. If you have good statistics that show incontrovertible evidence of higher temperatures and bigger storms worldwide, how long will this trend last? We can't know. It looks as if we are at the beginning of a major shift in global weather patterns that will become much worse in the coming years, but we may be simply seeing a natural fluctuation in average weather, a statistical fluke that will right itself over the coming decades. The changes we are seeing now could be just a decade-long hiccup in geological time. No one knows. You can pick and choose what you want to see and prove it statistically. There can be no absolute clarity in single events, single places, or single parameters.

A batting average is like a weather average. When a player steps up to the plate, you can't see his batting average. You can't point to it on his uniform or discern it from the way he holds the bat. It's not an object in time and space. A high batting average does not *cause* him to hit a double any more than climate change *causes* more storms and heat waves—climate change *is* more storms and heatwaves. Like average weather, there are no visual clues for a player's batting average that lead you to expect a particular outcome as he prepares to swing. But a batting average is a very real thing. It tells you what is most *likely* to happen. If you have to form an opinion or make a decision, it is beneficial to know the odds. To make a good decision, you have to believe in the reality of averages, even if you can't see them as physical objects. You have to be able to think about them and put them into the context of the bigger picture. Batting averages are more than interesting statistics; coaches rely upon them to determine the optimal batting order. When considering climate change, we need to see from the informed perspective of the team manager rather than an oblivious spectator in the stands. We need to become familiar with the odds.

Managing climate change requires exercising the human capacity for abstract thought.

I think the changes we are seeing in the weather now are the beginning of a major, long-term trend. The overwhelming likelihood is that temperatures will keep rising and there will be more storms, more severe storms, more droughts and fires, and an overall drop in agricultural production even as the population rises. I do not know how severe climate change will be, but I know that the more carbon we burn, the worse it will be. I know that. Climate change will be severe enough in the coming years for everyone to experience its existence on a first-hand basis. The trends we are seeing now are exactly what climate science has predicted they would be. That extra 48 percent CO_2 in the atmosphere is doing exactly what science said it would do. We can no longer prevent climate change. Our only hope is to prevent its worst effects by undertaking a radical, long-range strategy. This is essential. No matter how difficult it will be, we must act *radically*, we must act *immediately*, and we must *sustain* that action for the next several decades.

I think we should stop the combustion of all fossil fuels everywhere.

All of it.

No "cutting back"; no "reducing emissions"—stop *all* emissions.

How do we stop the combustion of fossil fuels? More importantly, who is the "we" that needs to do it? The government? The oil companies? The Ruling Class? I'll get to that soon. First, let us try to understand why this is happening now.

2

Why Is This Happening?

Here's something different:
Let's say nobody is doing anything wrong.

"Nobody is doing anything wrong."

Nobody sets out to ruin the habitability of the planet just to get rich. People are ruining the planet and getting rich in the process, but that's not what they set out to do. They just want to make money. Energetic, insightful, enterprising people set out to get rich, or just get by, by providing other people with artificial forms of energy that are needed to build and sustain modern civilization. For the most part, the build-up of carbon dioxide in the Earth's atmosphere is without evil intent. It is important to know this—to accept this truth—even if it is not true in all cases. Even if it is only mostly true. It is important because how effective we are in managing climate change depends on how we relate to other people.

Other people who do not agree.

How we relate to people who do not agree depends on how we understand their intentions.

Most people think they are doing good things. This is a good place to start.

Coal is good people.
Coal keeps the lights on.

It does. Coal really does keep the lights on. You can believe it. Without coal, we would be shivering in the dark. You can talk all you want about tornados and parts per million, but if you want heat and light, you know where to get it. Just flip the switch. We have to live now and we have to live with the resources available to us. If we want heat and light, food and transportation, we need coal.

There's a lot of logic here and a lot of truth. But the argument about climate is not about logic and truth—it's about the framework within which logic brings about truth, and there is more than one framework. Coal puts billions of tons of climate-busting carbon into the atmosphere. You can believe that, too. You can know that fossil fuel is existentially destructive as well as vital to civilized life as we know it. There is no contradiction. There is no violation of logic on either side and no "winning" the argument either way, no matter how watertight the logic. Even if you were to win the argument, what good would that do? The light switch on the wall would still be yours to flip.

100% REAL Update: November 19, 2018

The 100% Renewable Energy Alliance of Louisville introduced a resolution to the Louisville Metro Council that would require a step-by-step transition to renewable energy by 2030, 2035, and 2040. We have spoken with individual council members, to the entire council several times, and to members of the Parks and Sustainability Committee, where we made a major presentation. The president of the council initially sponsored the resolution but has since withdrawn; members of the committee have changed; a major budget crisis shifted attention away from less pressing matters; and we have withdrawn the resolution, temporarily. We will re-introduce it soon.

While the resolution was before the Parks and Sustainability Committee, I spoke one-on-one with a Republican member. Hurricane Michael had made landfall on the Florida panhandle five days earlier with winds of 155 mph, two mph short of a category five hurricane. In the area covered, and in total rainfall Michael was one of the largest storms ever to hit the U.S. mainland. (The President visited the area and claimed that winds had reached "almost 200 miles per hour.")

The committee member held up a copy of the resolution and said, "So this says you want to stop coal barge traffic on the Ohio River."

"No. It says we want to stop all new fossil fuel infrastructure, including coal barge traffic, by 2035. It won't happen tomorrow. But the infrastructure we build today is the infrastructure we are stuck with tomorrow. By 2035, everybody everywhere is going to be using renewable energy, so let's not build the wrong infrastructure today."

"And you think you can do that with a government resolution? Why, if solar is so wonderful, don't all these houses around here have solar panels on their rooftops? If people are going to save money, why haven't they installed panels on their homes? I'm a great believer in the market. Let the market do it, not the government. Why do we need to make people do what they don't want to do by passing resolutions like this?" He held the resolution up again, flipping it back and forth in the air dismissively. "I've been teaching economics for many years: if you want things to change you have to let the market do it."

"I agree. I am a great believer in the market," I responded. "I'm a businessman—the market gets me out of bed in the morning" (remembering my days running a construction crew). "But the market doesn't have eyes and ears. It can't see the wider world. When people stop at the gas pump or turn on a light switch, they are participating in the market, but they can't see what that does to the atmosphere. So we rely on the government to provide an overall direction within which the market can operate."

"But this resolution just tells people what they can't do. It just gums up the works. I know how these things go. You should see what it's like when builders complain to us about having to follow rules laid out by the city government."

17

"I know. I was a builder for a long time. I always complained when some guy with a tie and a clipboard showed up on the job site. I'm trying to get something done, and he's worried about checking off little boxes..."

"That's why I can't support this resolution the way it is." He interrupted. "I'm about what's practical. All those 'Whereases' just aren't going to make it."

"They can change in committee."

"You know what happens to these things: they get chewed up and spit out until they are no longer what they were." He pushed the resolution to one side.

"I'm not interested in that," I stated. And I'm not. The last thing I want is a toothless resolution providing cover for politicians.

"You better be ready for it. This is a left-wing city, but even so, I don't think this resolution has a chance."

"I'm not thinking left-wing/right-wing here." (I had never heard Louisville described in such terms.) "I'm thinking about what the real world is going to look like in 2035. What is practical in the future that we are really facing? Look out the window— out there—what kind of atmosphere are we going to have? What kind of weather? We're just now being hit with a new reality, over the last few years—the last few days. Who's going to protect against that? Who's going to take care of the forests and the oceans if it's cheaper to keep throwing junk out the window?" His head straightened and his eyes set back. He was listening. "Government is supposed to be all of us, as a whole, representing our interests as a whole. Are young people going to want to live and work in a city 17 years from now that's still burning fossil fuel?"

"If people want renewable energy, the market will serve them; not the government."

"We can create incentives that work with the market. When I started installing solar panels eleven years ago, they cost four or five times as much as they do now. With the 30 percent federal tax credit, the price for solar installation has come down enough

to create a larger market for panels. Manufacturers have realized efficiency of scale. That's why solar panels are so much cheaper now."

"I'd like to see you work with Habitat for Humanity or something like that, not try to get the whole city to go your way. I just can't support this the way it is." The councilman rose from his chair. "Thanks for coming in."

"Thank you for the work that you do. I understand you are not only a metro councilman but a teacher and a fire department major."

"Yup. Keeps me busy."

"Thank you for your service."

The controversy about climate change is the result of a conflict between worldviews, between unconscious frameworks within which people see and understand life. It's an argument between two sets of assumptions—two paradigms. One worldview believes—consciously or unconsciously—that the aim in life is making money. Operating under this perspective, we strive to make the best living we can for ourselves, for our family, and society as a whole. The world is primarily raw material for our use. The other worldview assumes—consciously or unconsciously—that the most important thing in life is life: plant, animal, and human. We are aware of our impact on nature and want to share the biosphere with plants and animals. We strive to sustain and protect life.

The first worldview, the *economic paradigm,* has dominated human civilization for centuries, especially in the United States. Economic development has been, and still is, the primary thrust of organized human life. The ecology is subservient to the economy. We preserve nature because we can afford to preserve nature. We preserve parklands because we want to have places to get away from it all. The second worldview, the *ecologic paradigm,* has come to the fore only recently, as human society begins to see the limits of economic growth. Only as the scale of human activity approaches the scale of biospheric activity are people seeing that the economy can be no larger than the ecology. The economy can exist only within the ecology. Humanity exists within the environment.

Either logic is based on the subconscious assumptions of the paradigm itself. Each worldview is "right" within its own logic. And because logic will never reveal the assumptions on which it is based, you cannot use your own logic to convince someone with an opposing worldview. You end up talking past him or her. How, then, do you convince anyone that the economy must adapt to accommodate the environment?

You don't.

You don't convince.
You show by example.

In an organized, systematic manner,
You stop buying carbon.

You don't have to be right to stop buying carbon.
You boycott carbon.

If you're going to have a boycott, you have to be against something. You need an enemy to take down. You have to aim the boycott at someone, don't you?

At whom do we aim the carbon boycott? You may think the answer is obvious.

The coal companies, of course! And the gas companies! And don't forget the oil companies! They are the largest corporations in the world! They make trillions on trillions of dollars with their drilling rigs in desert sands, in arctic tundras, and offshore, with their fracking operations scattered across the countryside, and with their tunneled out and topped off mountains. Their refineries pollute the atmosphere, their pipelines and waste impoundments pollute the rivers, and their money pollutes the political process in hundreds of legislatures around the world. Along with their noxious byproducts, fossil fuel companies funnel billions of tons of carbon dioxide and methane into the Earth's atmosphere. This is the enemy we seek! Let us shut down the fossil fuel industry!

But wait a minute.

Why do they do what they do? Why do hundreds of thousands of people who work in the coal, gas, and oil industries spend their careers wrecking the Earth? Why would they want to despoil the only place in the universe where we know we can live? Remember: they only sell what we buy. We're all complicit. Are we all so driven by base urges that we can't help choosing momentary comfort over long-term survival? Are we under the influence of an evil force? I don't believe in blaming evil. I choose not to invest my energy into a faulty scapegoat.

So who is accountable for climate change? It's the result of what humans—all of us, to one extent or another—are doing to the Earth. We don't have the moral high ground to assign blame to any external party, or substance. Even fossil fuels themselves, coal, oil, and natural gas, are not the enemy. They are (or at least were) quite good—extremely good—in fact, the best thing that has ever happened to human civilization.

Before fossil fuel, all food, buildings, and transportation (except for sailing vessels) were produced by the muscle power of people and draft animals. Ninety to one hundred percent of all people in all societies were devoted to food production. There was no central heating, no artificial lighting at the end of the workday, no air conditioning. There were no supermarkets, movies, TVs, computers, refrigerators, cars, highways, buses, airplanes, lawnmowers, snowmobiles, or tall buildings. No cold beer. Little of what we see, eat, or do was available before we began burning fossil fuel. We owe who we are to fossil fuel. To hate fossil fuel is to hate who we are. Hating who we are is not a solid foundation for accomplishing anything.

There is a force at play that manipulates our behavior and explains much of what is happening that seems beyond our control. Markets dictate the shots. There is nothing sinister about markets—they are not bad or good—but markets have no consciousness. The market is a muscle deep in the tissue of the body politic: a muscle that cannot see what it is doing to the larger world.

The market has no brain.

The market has no eyes or ears. It does not see an oil slick on the water or hear carbon dioxide bubbling up into the atmosphere. It does not care about glaciers melting in the arctic or about a coal miner's black lung. It's just a tool: a powerful tool. The market is the great blind, brainless, heartless muscle of the economy. We do not use *it*—it uses *us*, all the time. We humans are the great heart and brain of the economy, but we have never told the muscle just what we would like it to do. It just flexes—in and out, up and down, back and forth—mining, milling, manufacturing, and marketing stuff.

A boycott is the insertion of human consciousness into the market.

To carry out a successful boycott, we have to grab the market by the handle.

Consciousness is a vision of the possible and the real. Free of physical reality, vision can be anything and tends toward idealization. We see in our minds what we would like to see in the world. But a boycott, to be successful, reduces idealization to practical action by determining what can and should be accomplished in the real world. A boycott is always visionary and always doable. It has to motivate people to see the possible in their minds and bring it forth into the realm of reality.

"Money is the root of all evil."

No, it doesn't go that way. The saying is a bit longer:

"The *love* of money is the root of all evil."

And since we're not blaming evil, we can shorten it to:
"The love of money is the root...of the issue."

I like money, and I think we should keep using it. It is deeply
rooted in how people live together and there is no way we could stop
using it. But we should not love it. We should not worship the market, and that's what we do in the United States. My people bow down
before the market.

We worship the market because it does so much for us. It saves
us. It sustains us. When resources seemed unlimited and civilization was fully contained in the biosphere, the market was how we
reconciled our working lives with our spending lives. The market
told us where work was needed and which supplies were the cheapest and most abundant. Without bureaucracy, without commands
from a legislature, a king, or a dictator, the "invisible hand" of the
market told us who was needed, and where, for what purpose. When
more lumberjacks or lawyers were needed, consumer demand for
lumber or legal work created higher salaries for people who could
chop down trees or write legal briefs. The consumer act of buying
more lumber and less brick, or more legal work and less medical
work, led to higher prices that stimulated investment and employment where it was most needed. Nobody had to figure out what was
needed: the price for the most in-demand services and goods just
went up. Careers were built where the money was, and consumers
got the stuff they wanted most. No government, no taxes, no bum-
bling bureaucrats. Efficient operations survived; the inefficient went
out of business, and the economy soared. The market system was
financially satisfying and intellectually satisfying. The market was
the final arbiter of winners and losers and the world of economics
mirrored the world of biological survival of the fittest.

We still do as the market commands. We still bow down. The market decides for us on all decisions, collective and individual, major and
minor. Do I buy this car or that car? Do I look for work here or there?

Do we build a new bridge or a new airport? What is the cost-benefit analysis? What is the payback period? Which way will I end up with more money? All this is as it should be—we should be careful with money—but when we fall down before the god of the market, we no longer control our actions. We no longer look at what we are doing. The forests can fall, the seas dry up, and the air turn black while we are blindly following the dictates of supply and demand.

I say the market has become a god because of the praise we shower upon it, the control we allow it over our lives, and the power it has over our thinking. We know how it works, but we don't know what it *is*. Like any god, the market is invisible; we see what it does, but we do not see it in our midst. It guides us at a subconscious level, but we are often unaware of its prompting. We can see it at work when we think about buying solar panels or an electric car, and our minds automatically ask a series of questions. How much does it cost? How much will I save? Is there a cheaper way? These are good questions and we should consider the answers, but we should also see beyond them. There's a bigger world out there. We should acknowledge the market and be thankful for it, but shape it to our advantage—not worship it. We should look beyond the market and *use* its powers to do what needs to be done. To live sustainably on the Earth, we will inject consciousness into the power of the market.

100% REAL. Update: June 6, 2019

Today we received a solid endorsement from the Bonnycastle Neighborhood Association (a group I spoke to briefly a couple of days ago) for the 100 percent renewable energy resolution.

The resolution was heard in the Parks and Sustainability Committee of the Louisville Metro Council this afternoon. Ten people from 100% REAL were present, and we expected a vote. But after some discussion centering on the availability of viable alternatives to coal and natural gas, the committee decided not to vote without further study. A representative of the utility company

(LG&E) reminded committee members of a study completed by her company demonstrating the impact of complete reliance on renewables. I read the study several months ago. Its findings were preposterous, suggesting at one point that a large adjoining city park would have to be completely covered with solar panels for the neighborhood to supply its own energy.

I had hoped for a quick passage of the resolution, but upon consideration, I am glad the committee is taking this resolution seriously. We have been speaking at Metro Council meetings for 10 months now, and they may have begun to listen. Or they may have begun to listen to the weather report.

3

Timetable for the End of Fossil Fuel

Homo Sapiens	200,000 years
Agriculture	10,000 years
Civilization (Cities)	5500 years
Fossil Fuels	200 years
Now	Marginal Climate Change
End of Fossil Fuel Age	30 years from now

Meanwhile: June 25, 2019

The temperature today in Paris, France, reached 109 Fahrenheit, 5 degrees hotter than the previous record.

Too much carbon in the atmosphere will mean the end of human civilization as we know it. The end of agriculture, literacy, division of labor, and urbanized human settlement. Humanity is hundreds of thousands of years old, but agriculture evolved only within the last ten thousand years during a period of climate stability after the last ice age. Our cities (permanent settlements, writing, division of labor) are only 5,000 years old. Humans as hunters and farmers have known climate change many times over, but *civilization* has never known it, and civilization will not survive severe agricultural losses due to changes in temperature and rainfall. Humanity in some form—in some diminished form—will likely survive the current climate crisis, but human civilization will not. Until the last few thousand years, people were able to keep the species alive by migrating from one climate zone to another or by changing lifestyle in place. Hunter-gatherers were able to find new sources of sustenance in the same habitat or move to nearby habitats as the climate changed gradually over the centuries and decades. Changes in the climate were slow enough to allow gradual adaptation over generations. People alive then may never have noticed changes in average weather. But now, as most of the Earth's arable land is fully developed for agriculture and all of the Earth's habitable land is divided and claimed by sovereign authorities, there is no room for mass migration. There are thousands of times as many people now, and no new places to start civilization over from scratch. Furthermore, because the climate is changing so rapidly, there is no time for in-place adaptation.

So it's not human extinction we are worried about. Most likely, there will be survivors, perhaps large numbers of them, eking out a living in various parts of the world. What we are worried about is the viability of reestablishing a settled way of life with permanent houses, jobs, agriculture, manufacturing, arts, learning, and culture.

The future of civilization depends on eliminating all atmospheric carbon dioxide emissions.

But how?

Life moves forward. We cannot go backward to the Pleistocene Epoch (Ice Age). We would make lousy Paleolithic hunters even if the big game were still around. But life as we know if cannot go forward burning fossil fuel, either. We have to stop. If we go forward at all, it will be forward in an entirely new direction. But who will "we" be, as modern human beings? Who will we be without all of the things we have become since we started burning fossil fuel? Good question!

We've already acknowledged that our civilization has co-evolved recently with coal, oil, and natural gas, and we will need more of these fuels to continue living what now seems a "normal" lifestyle. We should now recognize that we are more than our reliance on fossil fuel. We humans go back way before fossil fuel. We are much more than a mindless blob of protoplasm chomping on coal and oil, belching and flatulating climate-busting gases. We were a viable life form before 1820. We survived as humans for hundreds of thousands of years, and as *civilized* humans for thousands of years, before fossil fuels made their appearance in our midst. As humans, we have the innate capacity to evolve. This doesn't have to be the final chapter of our story. We can continue to develop as a species and band together in our intention to put the use of fossil fuels firmly in our past.

This may seem too hopeful. It may sound a bit trite. But if we do not rise to the occasion, this *may* be the final chapter in our story. I don't want to talk about that. I don't want to talk about what will happen if we don't change our ways and burn up all the fossil fuel the Earth has to offer. It's too scary. Scary stuff gets our attention (it really could happen) but it makes us feel bad about ourselves and does not inspire creativity. Instead of fear, we need confidence. We need to believe we can do what we need to do. So the first step is to understand that civilization can take on an entirely new form. We don't easily change who we are, but we have done it in the past and can do it again. We should see our society now as being in a state of transition away from the use of fossil fuels. They have been around for only a short time (about 200 years) and they will be gone soon. We had cities and learning and arts and religion and voyages of discovery and all that good stuff way before we had coal or oil or gas, and we will have all these good things again when we no longer have coal and oil and gas. Dependence on fossil fuel is just a phase we are going through.

100% REAL: Update: July 22, 2019

Together with another constituent, I met with my metro council representative today. He had expressed interest and support when we introduced the resolution for 100 percent renewable energy last year, but without enthusiasm. Like many council members, he did not feel that a resolution would have much meaning because it would be nonbinding. Nobody would pay attention to it once it passed. (Another council member we spoke to assured us that the resolution would not pass because it would "bind" the city to unrealistic goals.)

Nevertheless, we persisted. After an hour or so of back and forth, my councilman agreed to not only vote for the resolution but to sponsor it. Furthermore, he is chairman of the Public Works Committee and expects to have it introduced into his committee.

We've been burning coal for a long time as a supplement to firewood, but we did not start burning it in significant amounts until the industrial revolution was fully underway in 1880. That is the first year a measurable increase in carbon dioxide can be detected in the atmosphere. A generation or so later, with the advent of the automobile, people began burning significant amounts of petroleum. And in the last two or three generations, natural gas has been used for heating buildings, manufacturing fertilizer, drying grain, and generating electricity. These fuels are compact, portable, cheap, and abundant; we have built an entire civilization around them. From an historical perspective, it's amazing how quickly we have adapted to fossil fuels and how quickly they have transformed every aspect of our lives. Nobody knew they would change the climate.

Nobody knew they would change the climate.

Nobody is to blame.

Everyone is to blame, if anyone. And what good is that?

Fossil fuels are an addiction. We can't stop using them and we can't survive without them. We are dependent on them and our reliance is hurting the planet. But fossil fuels are also the catalyst that got modern civilization going. They have brought us from the horse and buggy days to the space age. They have taken the human species in a direction no living form has ever taken before. Fossil fuels have shifted the course of human development for all time and altered the choreography of biological evolution for all living beings.

A Quick History of the Climate

The problem began 10,000 years ago. The Ice Age was over, the great glaciers had melted, and the climate was cool, pleasant, and stable, or what we, as fully evolved Homo sapiens, consider cool, pleasant, and stable. We got hooked on a stable climate. The climate became dependable enough over the years, decades and centuries, to make the planting of seeds and tending of crops a good investment of time and human energy. Where people before had worked in the moment to gather what nature provided, people now worked many months in advance of the payback, digging soil, pulling weeds, and carrying water in the hope of a harvest. In the long run, if the weather cooperated, the harvest was much better with agriculture than with gathering. Agriculture was a good investment—a wonderful investment that paid off many times over. A family could produce more food farming than they could themselves eat; this allowed them to sell the excess to pay taxes and buy things they could not make themselves. Enough food stored for the off-season meant an end to ceaseless wandering for food; it meant the possibility of settling down in one place. Agricultural surplus meant villages and cities. It meant non-agricultural classes: craftsmen, scribes, priests, soldiers, shopkeepers, and bureaucrats. Not everybody had to be a farmer. But it also meant a society-wide dependence on the agricultural surplus, which meant dependence on a stable climate. Agriculture does not like surprises.

Nearly all the Earth's land suitable for agriculture is now under cultivation.

Human civilization exists within and continues to depend on a stable climate.

Changes in temperature and rainfall will result in lower food production.

If we were still hunter-gatherers we would not have much to worry about with climate change.

The climate has been so stable over the last 10,000 years that civilization has come to take it for granted. Our society revolves around the expectation of relative climate stability. As the climate becomes less stable our relationship with the natural world will change. We will no longer be a passive witness of the weather. We will become part of it.

We will become part of the weather.

We inadvertently began to influence the Earth's weather system around 1880, when we began burning enough coal heating houses, powering factories, and driving trains to increase the overall carbon dioxide content of the atmosphere. CO_2 was 280 ppm at that time. Now it is 417 ppm (2020). Enacting the carbon boycott, carbon taxes, cap and trade, and other renewable energy strategies in the near future would be a proactive form of human influence intended to have a positive impact on the climate. Perhaps viable forms of *extracting* CO_2 from the atmosphere will become yet another way that we enter the finer workings of the weather system. Our involvement is permanent. From now on we will be part of how the weather behaves. We will tend the Earth's atmosphere in the future as we have tended her soil in the past. There will never be a point in the future when the problem will be solved and we will be able to go back to a simpler time when steering the climate was not our worry. The carbon boycott may end, the climate may one day stabilize, but we will be tending the atmosphere from now on. We will not control it; we will *tend* it: by curbing emissions, by removing carbon, or even by adding carbon back in at some point. "Carbon policy" will become an aspect of global management.

How did I arrive at the 30-year timeframe by which I propose that we aim to be off fossil fuel completely? In October of 2018, the United Nations' Intergovernmental Panel on Climate Change (IPCC) issued a special report: "Global Warming of 1.5°C." Where previous IPCC studies had concentrated on a global temperature rise of 2.0° Celsius, this report showed that a 1.5°C rise would be much less damaging. A mere half-degree difference in average temperatures would have far-reaching consequences and prevent the worst of what we have to fear from climate change. But even a 1.5°C degree rise over preindustrial temperatures will result in food shortages, droughts, wildfires, heat waves, hurricanes, tornadoes, extinctions, and the massive die-off of coral reefs. Many of the weather effects previously thought to kick in at 2.0° now seem likely to occur as we reach 1.5° around 2040. (Temperatures are already up by about 1.0°.)

The report was written and edited by 91 scientists from 40 countries who analyzed more than 6,000 scientific studies. To prevent 1.5° degrees of warming, the report says greenhouse pollution must be reduced by 45 percent by 2030, and 100 percent by 2050. In this study, the world's leading climate scientists warn that after 2030 there will be no way to prevent less than a maximum of 1.5° rise, and a half degree more than 1.5° will significantly worsen droughts, floods, and extinctions, as well as increase the likelihood of poverty for hundreds of millions of people. A half-degree less warming would also prevent corals from disappearing, reduce sea-level rise, and decrease the loss of sea ice in the arctic.

Now if I thought there might be a threat to my way of life and that of my family, friends, community, nation, and the world, I would want to learn everything I could about exactly what that threat was. And I would want to know what I could do about it. I would get an appointment with the United Nations and ask to have 91 scientists from 40 nations read through 6000 recent studies on the subject, boil it down to a single comprehensive picture, and present that picture to the world with recommendations as to what could be done. I would pick scientists because scientists are a skeptical and contentious lot, always trying to disprove each others' theories. If 91 of them can agree on anything, there must be something real out there. I would pick the

United Nations and I would pick scientists, which is exactly what has been done. The conclusions have been presented to the world for our use.

> Half of the carbon by 2030,
> All of it by 2050.

!!

Is anybody listening?

The IPCC report notes that climate damage will be irreversible. Once we get above 1.5° or 2.0° rise, it will be nearly impossible to get back down for centuries, perhaps millennia, even if carbon dioxide levels come down. Even if we mend our ways sometime after 2030 or 2050, we will not be able to get back to the climate we have had for the last 10,000 years. We have to make the change now. This is due to a variety of factors, including the *delayed effect* of greenhouse gases, and *positive feedback loops*.

As of yet, we have seen only slight effects from the 48 percent increase in atmospheric CO_2 levels, because billions of tons of new carbon (most of it) have been absorbed by the oceans. The oceans can hold a lot more carbon than the air and have so far prevented the worst impacts. But the oceans are becoming saturated. As more and more CO_2 is absorbed in water, more dissolves into carbonic acid (H_2CO_3), which raises the acidity of the entire oceanic system. (The effect has been slight until recently, but now threatens marine life, especially coral and shellfish.)

In holding so much CO_2 out of the atmosphere, the oceans have delayed the effect of atmospheric emissions on the weather. This is good in that it gives us time to figure out what to do before the catastrophe happens, but bad in that it has kept us from seeing *in real-time* the effects of what we are doing. I have always felt that the changes we make in the way we live will not happen until people witness firsthand what the climate is doing. They will have to feel the heat, experience the fires, suffer through the droughts, and watch their own crops and towns flooding before they realize the severity of what is happening. Reading about what might happen in the future is not enough. The delaying effect of oceanic absorption of excess atmospheric carbon has interfered with our ability to see what we are doing and lulled us into blindness and apathy. The climate change we are experiencing now is from the fuels we burned 20 or 30 years ago, and what we are burning now will affect the weather a generation from now. Even if people around the world succeed in eliminating all future carbon emissions, what we are burning now and storing in the oceans will continue to damage the biosphere for centuries to come.

The other irreversible effect of today's carbon emissions is due to *positive feedback loops.* In heating the atmosphere a little bit now, we cause much worse heating in the future, even if we stop carbon emissions entirely at some point. There are several types of positive feedback loops. The first is the well-known *albedo* effect: a slight warming in Polar regions leads to marginal ice melt. Ice reflects sunlight, sending 90 percent of incoming solar radiation back into space; but melting ice exposes dark, open seawater, which *absorbs* incoming sunlight, further warming the water and the air. More warming leads to more melting, more open seawater, and yet more warming. The cycle perpetuates itself (hence, the "positive" feedback). Notice here that carbon emissions are no longer the problem. Once the feedback kicks in, it keeps going on its own. The carbon we add to the atmosphere triggers the loop.

Another positive feedback loop is melting arctic soils. Warming due to carbon emissions melts the permafrost releasing methane, carbon dioxide, and other greenhouse gases previously frozen in the soil. Once in the atmosphere, these gases trap more solar radiation and cause more warming, which melts more permafrost, etc., etc. Both the albedo and permafrost feedback loops are already in effect to some extent. A potentially much worse feedback loop that is not yet in effect is the methane hydrate loop. Millions of tons of methane lie frozen deep below the ocean floor. Were they ever to melt, they would cause a rapid rise in global temperatures and likely a mass extinction.

Methane hydrate feedback loops are, in fact, prime suspects in some of the mass extinction events of the distant past.

Some feedback loops are negative, working against temperature changes and helping to stabilize the climate when it tends too far in one direction or another. Photosynthesis is an example of a negative loop. Because plants use carbon dioxide to build carbohydrates, higher CO_2 levels increase rates of photosynthesis and remove excess carbon from the atmosphere, cooling things back down. This has been one of the Earth's foremost means of self-regulation. It would be effective now if we were not cutting down tropical forests much faster than they are growing back. Worldwide, photosynthesis is currently decreasing, not increasing. Droughts, fires, and deforestation are increasing carbon levels more rapidly than photosynthesis can decrease them.

This will make interesting reading in the coming years. We know where we stand, or think we know. What better source of information could there be? Nobody knows for sure what the future will bring—it might be worse, it might be not so bad, the IPCC could be off by a year or two—but these 6000 climate studies summarized by 91 scientists are the best information we have at this point. What more accurate way could exist to provide us with concrete details about the future we face?

100% REAL Update: July 26, 2019

> *I called the executive director of Bernheim Forest today. Bernheim is a woodland preserve of several thousand acres just south of Louisville. I called the director to talk about a problem they are having. The local utility company wants to cut a 75-foot right-of-way through the preserve and install a natural gas pipeline. The particular part of the preserve is a recent purchase; Bernheim buys land and accepts donated land specifically for conservation. Deed restriction and conservation easements legally protect the land from development of any sort. Nature preserves are not preserves unless they are legally protected. The local utility*

company threatens to use eminent domain to condemn the land in order to build their pipeline. They claim that heightened consumer demand requires additional infrastructure. A Louisville Gas and Electric spokesman had this to say: "There is concern from Bullitt County economic officials that there could be a period of no growth in the community, as a result of any delay, and that's why we're working to move forward because we know there is demand and need."

There are a lot of issues here that interest me. I don't know what to do to help, but I will be going to Bernheim next week to get a closer look.

4

So Much for Talk.
How Do We Walk the Walk?

The way to stop burning fossil fuel is to stop buying it.

We're going to stop buying it.
We're going to boycott carbon.

Simple.

If carbon fuels are the problem, the solution is no more carbon fuels.

Got it?

All you do is do it.

Let's consider our current reliance on fossil fuels in our homes.

Power lines are strung overhead, the car is waiting in the driveway, gas lines connect under the street somewhere, and the lights are on. We're just sitting here listening to refrigerators, fans, and furnaces kicking on and off.

How do we shut all this down?

As an experiment, it might be a good idea to try not using anything that runs on fossil fuels someday—but not on a cold day. Just turn everything off. Don't drive the car. Don't use the computer ... or even the phone. Don't mow the lawn. Don't open the fridge. Don't use the stove. Don't wear anything manufactured by power machinery. Don't eat anything produced by tractors or artificial fertilizers or transported by truck or train. Just try it for a day, if only in your mind.

This is the starting point. Everything proceeds from here. The boycott proceeds not from having all this stuff, but from not having it. Fossil fuel is not the alternative to the boycott; the alternative is no fuel at all.

Not having any energy at all is the starting point.

Deciding that fossil fuel is not an option, even when available, is the key to a successful carbon boycott. This means that the alternative to implementing renewable energy is having no fuel. With this in mind, we can start re-building a new economy. What this means is that renewable energy will not do all the same things for us as carbon fuel—we won't simply shift from one fuel to another—we will have to adapt to whatever renewable energy *can* do for us. There is no point in comparing the benefits of renewables vis-à-vis fossil fuel. The comparison is between renewable energy and no energy. Renewables might not be as good as carbon or they might be better, but whatever they are, we have to adapt to them. To live on, we have to adapt. That's all there is to it.

We should not, then, begin with our current use of natural gas, electricity, and gasoline. We should not think in terms of pulling the plug from fossil fuels and inserting the same plug into the sun and the wind and the Earth. It may not work that way. We may have to change how we live. We may not be able to go wherever we want to go, whenever we want to go; we may not have a wide variety of food to choose from; we may have a role in producing the food we eat. Times might be hard. On the other hand, there might be goods and conveniences available with renewable energy that we don't have now. But either way, we are going to have to make the transition, and it may or may not be smooth. It may not be a transition at all, if, by *a transition*, we mean simply finding another way to have all the things we have now. We may have to spend some time in the cold. Or we may find it's not so bad.

100% REAL Update: August 8, 2019

The resolution for 100 percent renewable energy was read again to the Louisville Metro Council. It was not assigned to the Public Works Committee as expected, but assigned once again to the Parks and Sustainability Committee, which failed to pass it last year. Judging by its title, the Parks and Sustainability Committee should be receptive to a renewable energy proposal, but the membership of the committee does not seem progressively-minded. They are scheduled to meet next week.

Meanwhile: August 8, 2019

The IPCC came out with another report today, "Climate Change and Land," concerning agriculture and forestry. Over 100 scientists from 52 countries looked at 7000 climate studies. They found that today's agriculture and forestry practices produce 23 percent of total greenhouse gas emissions. That's a lot. Even if we stop burning all fossil fuels immediately but fail to change how we eat and what we grow, climate change will continue to climb towards 2.0° C and beyond. However, the fact that meat production uses up so much more land than plant-based food production creates a grand opportunity to cut back on carbon build-up. Photosynthesis (a negative feedback loop that exerts a positive effect on the climate) is the best natural mechanism we have for reducing carbon. If people were to eat less meat, millions of acres of cultivated land could be restored to forestland, which would absorb billions of tons of carbon from the atmosphere. How do we quantify "less?" Eating less meat is not eliminating all meat from my diet. I eat mostly plants, but I'll wolf down a burger now and again: is that good enough? Or, if I'm talking about eliminating all carbon, do I have to eliminate all meat, too? Are we still looking for consistency here?

Civilization cannot survive using fossil fuel to supply its needs. Burning coal, oil, and natural gas cannot continue under any circumstances. We will use renewable energy or no energy, but how do we get to that future from where we are now?

Let us stand in the cold for a day, or just a minute, or just a thought, and turn everything off: the car, the fridge, the furnace, the lights—everything—and then, one by one, figure out how to turn each back on again, if we can, using renewable energy. And let's allow ourselves a few years to figure out how we can do this. Let's realize right now—this minute—that we have to do this. Let us take a few days or months to think things through, then let's commit to a long-term, multi-decade transition away from all forms of fossil fuel to new forms of renewable energy: a complete make-over. We're taking a chance here—we can't know all the details now—but we're betting that there will be ways to turn all or most of the things we need back on again with renewable energy. If for some reason, there are some things we can't turn back on again, we will have to do without them. Maybe we just think we need them. One way or another, we will have to adapt to the cold, hard facts of physical reality. It might be fun.

One way to stop using fossil fuel is to go back to the good old days. Don't figure out how to turn things back on again. Get rid of them. Get rid of cars, factories, refrigerators, thermostats, and monoculture farming. Walk, ride a horse, cut your own firewood, grow your own food. Some of this may become necessary, whether desirable or not. People used to live this way and lived pretty well. Fossil fuel might seem "necessary" for life, but it's not. We lived without it for centuries and can do without it again. George Washington was carbon neutral. We could go back there if we had to.

But we don't, and we won't.

As mentioned previously, life is not designed to move backward. There's a ratcheting response to human invention and biological evolution overall. Against a background of randomness, the arrow of time points toward higher levels of order. Once we get used to something we like, it's hard to give it up. Luxuries become necessities. Inventions become needs. We forget how to raise horses and grow food. We don't want to raise horses and grow food. There is a much better chance of finding energy from renewable sources than there is of going back to the good old days.

But…

The knowledge that we *could* go backward, if we really had to, may prove important—just knowing that it's an option. Learning to live more simply may become a survival skill for the critical transitional period. We may have to learn to fix old things and grow a few rows of beans. Warm clothing may become more reliable than adjusting a thermostat to "room temperature." (Room temperature is an example of a very recent luxury, now considered a need by many.) Many people may learn to like living more simply and closer to the natural world. Doing so may come to seem more like moving forward than backward. We may redefine our needs to fit within the parameters of what we can provide for ourselves.

It's good to know that simple living has been done before and we can do it again if we have to.

We will have to go backward, I think, to an extent.

But the main thrust will be forward. There will be solar panels, electric cars, driverless cars, windmills, electric trucks and tractors, community-based organic farming, smaller homes, bio-fueled or hydrogen-fueled aircraft and home heating, and geothermal heating and cooling. Eventually, citywide deep geothermal may become a practical energy source, and solar collection may become possible in low Earth orbit. There is no way to predict what the future holds. Thirty years ago, who could have foreseen cell phones? First, we can redefine our needs within the context of a practical transition to renewable energy, and from there we can move forward with one-part strategic retreat to every two-parts technological innovation.

To find what our actual fuel needs are, the starting point cannot be an assessment of our needs, which in our society we tend to conflate with our wants. The starting point has to be an understanding of the carrying capacity of the Earth and the consideration of the other humans and species that inhabit it along with us. We can do better than just survive. We can live well, have fun, feel good, and take care of the oceans, forests, and atmosphere if we start thinking of ways to do it. We can make sure there are enough planetary resources for all humans to live well, and all creatures survive and thrive. And we can do it by taking less for ourselves, by using less fossil fuels now with a commitment to eliminating use entirely by 2050.

The goal is not going to be achieved tomorrow. Let's give ourselves 10 or 20 or 30 years. No cold turkey; no crash diets: 10–30 years; 2030 to 2050. That gives us enough time to change incrementally. Wait until we need a new car or a new furnace or a new house. Make the big change then. Aim toward no carbon at all.

Why no fossil fuel at all? Won't there be a few appropriate uses of petroleum or natural gas on a very small scale? Of course there will: we're talking about the real world here. Of course there will be exceptions. But the goal will be an end to *all* fossil fuel everywhere, not a partial cutback. Partial cutbacks will not do the trick. There's so much carbon being dumped into the air now, so many billions of tons, that every little bit hurts. We have to recognize this and set our sights as high as they need to be to get us through this. Then allow a little leniency, just because we are fallible humans. I'm not sure this makes sense, but I am sure it is practical. Aim to get rid of all the coal, all the natural gas, and all the petroleum, then don't be surprised or dismayed if little leaks through the cracks. The atmosphere can take that much.

The difference between *aiming to reduce* carbon usage and *eliminating it* is psychologically significant. It is a matter of where you intend to go. If you're reducing emissions, you're still in the fossil fuel age trying to make a better fossil fuel age. If you're eliminating carbon, you've left the fossil age behind and are trying to clean up the mess it left behind. Cutting back a few percentage points on carbon fuels would be continuing to depend on them for our needs without changing our needs. It would be like quitting smoking, except when you really want a cigarette. To quit smoking, you have to think of yourself as a non-smoker. We have to begin thinking of ourselves as people who do not use coal, gasoline, and natural gas. If somebody sneaks a smoke out in the barn somewhere, well … we're only human. We have to find ways to get what we need without any fossil fuel at all. And then cut ourselves a little slack.

Consistency, by the way, is the refuge of small minds. Somebody said that, or something like that, maybe Emerson. And if he didn't, I did.

Now, what if 91 scientists from 40 countries turn out to be wrong? What if it only looks like we are hurtling toward climate disaster? What if it really is a hoax? It's not a hoax. A hoax would require the careful coordination of millions of people and a common motive. What would the motive be? Money? Prestige? Notoriety? I don't think so. There's not much of any of that in the climate business. I have to admit that there is a certain closeness you feel with other people who see what you see and go out of their way to do something about it. And I have to admit that once you begin to see the patterns of climate change, you tend to see them everywhere, even where they are not. But this is not a conspiracy theory. There's some real science out there. We didn't dream up a global-scale catastrophe just to put one over on the status quo.

It's not a hoax, but what if it's just plain wrong? What if there's something else going on that we can't see now? What if things aren't so bad and we could, without any ill effects on the climate, keep burning fossil fuels for as long as they last? It's possible—unlikely, but possible. If that were the case, we would look pretty stupid wasting 10–30 years undermining civilization, getting rid of the very things we most need. The greatest waste of effort in all history!

What would it be like? What if we get rid of all fossil fuels and then find out they never had any harmful effects on the climate? We would be in the embarrassing position of living for the rest of the century without oil spills, methane leaks, gas leaks, coal ash spills, black lung, sulfur dioxide pollution, disappearing resources, and wars fought over oil. No mercury polluted streams, no fracking wells, no pipelines or access roads cutting through wilderness areas, no topless mountains, and no smokestacks. No ozone on hot summer days. No coal trains, gas explosions, or supertankers. No running out of finite resources and no dependence on foreign fuel. We would be stuck with dependence on unlimited, free wind, solar, and geothermal energy. The "fuel" would be free and unlimited. In fact, there would be no fuel. Energy would no longer require fuel.

That would be the worst thing that could happen if we were to stop using all fossil fuels. Everywhere. By mistake.

So let's take a chance…

So far, those of us combatting the climate crisis have concentrated on taking three actions:

1. Protesting against the companies who extract, transport, and sell fossil fuels
2. Protesting against government policies that encourage fossil fuel use and lobbying for government policies that encourage renewable energy
3. Trying to use less fossil fuel in our personal lives

We have to keep taking all of these steps. The carbon boycott is not intended to replace any of these essential tactics. It's an additional action. So how is a boycott different from trying to use less fossil fuels in our personal lives? The carbon boycott combines public activism and private commitment into an organized economic force. We're not just each doing "our part" to slow the growth of carbon emissions by individual efforts to turn the thermostat down, drive less, or buy carbon credits when we travel by airplane—we're creating what the economists call *aggregate demand* for new forms of energy. By boycotting carbon, we're not asking for anything; we're not lobbying for anything; we're not suggesting anything—we're just not buying any more coal, oil, and natural gas. We're organizing and altering our buying behavior in a concerted way that will force the economy to adapt.

The key elements in a successful carbon boycott are:

- Organization
- Commitment
- Alternative Energy Sources

Organization

Organization means groups: small groups, large groups, city, national, and global groups, and groups within groups. Mostly it means people on the local level who know each other or want to get to know each other, people who like to work together, party together, and trust each other with their commitment to the cause. Groups can be formal (dues, monthly meetings, programs, etc.), informal (keep in touch, meet occasionally), or parts of other groups (a committee or side interest in an environmental group, civic association, church, synagogue, neighborhood association, hiking club, etc.). Groups of friends, mostly. Drinking buddies, maybe. Some new groups will form just for the boycott, but most will be groups that have already formed for other purposes: bridge clubs, supper clubs, book clubs, etc. The object should be for people to support each other and remain united over time. All actual commitments should be made on the individual level. The group should provide encouragement, knowledge, contacts, and education, but there should be no peer pressure to conform to a particular doctrine. The group can invite speakers, gather information, form a co-op or a buying group, pool resources, or secure community rates for solar or geothermal installation. But mostly, the group should reinforce the goals of individuals within it.

Groups that focus on the carbon boycott can have other over-lapping purposes. One might be social, another recreational, or spiritual. Energy use can be a pretty dry topic after a while, and energy use itself will not be the primary interest of most people in the boycott group. Members will gather to discuss better ways to live in harmony with the natural world and to develop a vision of society as a whole living within the carrying capacity of the Earth. People like to dream collectively. Groups can offer a place for collective dreaming, a place where friends can discuss what they see happening around them and what they would like to see happening. Dreaming is not the opposite of doing; dreaming is where doing begins. All practical applications begin with dreaming. Architects, engineers, and city planners are all dreamers. The vision of humanity living responsibly within the wider world of the living Earth is the most practical dream ever dreamt.

Local groups should be large enough for a diversity of views and small enough for people to know each other. Groups may grow, merge, divide, dwindle, and reproduce. They should stay in contact with other similar groups and stay in contact with umbrella groups on the national and global level. Mostly, group members will know what to do on the local level: build new houses and buy old houses with south facing roofs; drive an electric car or no car; eat locally; avoid single-use containers; install solar and geothermal; don't buy *stuff*; push for community solar and renewable energy utilities; fight pipelines; divest from fossil fuel companies; etc. But there should be some overall national and global direction to the boycott. The purpose of local groups is to help individuals through the transformation to a fossil-free future. The purpose of the carbon boycott on national and global levels is to diminish large-scale aggregate demand for fossil energy and to create conscious aggregate demand for renewable energy.

The keyword here is *conscious*. Too often when we buy something we do not think about where the product comes from, how it is made, what it is made from, and what its environmental impact may be. But to boycott carbon effectively, we will have to know what alternatives are available and in what sense they are truly alternative. Is natural gas, for instance, a viable alternative to coal? In a way, it is: it burns much cleaner and has only half the carbon content. But it still has carbon and quite a lot. It's still a fossil fuel. And fracking for natural gas has extreme environmental impacts. Natural gas may be better than coal and might be used to a limited extent during the transition period, but it is by no means a final answer.

There are also things to consider when it comes to renewable energy alternatives. People will soon find out that labeling fossil fuels "bad" and renewable energy sources "good" is too simplistic. Every form of energy has drawbacks. Solar panels use rare earth metals often mined in far off places. Wind turbines kill birds. Geothermal systems disturb a lot of soil. But, as in any real-world decision-making, people must weigh the cost versus the benefit. What we should avoid in boycott groups is puritanism: the tendency among some to imagine a perfect world and then obstruct any movement in the real world that does not conform to their sense of perfection. The perfect becomes the enemy of the good. We should look at the imperfections in renewable energy sources and weigh them against the problems caused by fossil fuels. Maybe we're using too much energy—whether fossil or renewable—overall. Maybe there are ways of softening environmental and social impacts. Maybe new engineering and manufacturing methods will improve or eliminate impacts. Maybe we should not be fighting too many battles at the same time.

One impact I, as a solar installer, run up against is the social inequality my industry creates. If you have the money (and good roof exposure), you can install solar on your house and have all the electricity you need for heating, cooling, lighting, cooking, and so forth—even for driving a car or two. But if you're struggling just to make rent payments, buy shoes for the kids, and eat at the same time, you might be looking at the people with solar panels as a privileged elite. They say solar saves money in the long run, but you don't have the long run. You have the end of the month. This is a new problem created by solar energy. (There are ways around this problem, but I will not get into that just now.) What I mean to say here is that we should fight one battle at a time. We should maintain the vision of a more equal society but not let that vision immobilize renewable energy installation now. At this stage, people with money are better able to make the transition than people without. That's not okay, but it's real. We have to move ahead with it. In time, we will have community solar, utility-scale solar, or some other way to democratize the distribution of renewable energy, but right now we have to get as much installed as possible. Since I began installing solar twelve years ago, the price of solar panels has come down to about a fifth of what it was, largely because of the economy of scale created by the early adopters of the technology, which were people who could afford it. Solar power is now available to people with more moderate incomes because enough people with the means to invest in solar early on did so. So listen to what the puritans have to say, then do what you can do now.

Another problem with puritanism is that opponents can get hold of it and twist it back on you. I hear all the time from climate deniers that we shouldn't go solar because it uses rare earth metals mined in China or because we will have to recycle used panels one day. In the Kentucky legislature last year solar opponents tried to distract the public away from renewable energy concerns by pitting the interests of "average hardworking" people against "rich solar" people. Listen to what opponents say, and then do what you have to do.

Commitment

With an organized boycott, the aggregate effect will be national and global. But the commitment to the cause should remain personal. The only form of enforcement should be the positive reinforcement individuals feel from the group. Commitment should be considered, gradual, and long-term. *Multi-decade* long-term. Enthusiastic? Sure, but sustained. Maintaining commitment is going to be hard, and probably lifelong. Avoid burn out.

There are a few things you can do right away: turn out lights, drive less, buy less, turn the thermostat down in winter and up in summer, recycle bottles and cans, etc. These are important steps, and help you develop the frame of mind you will need to move into a new lifestyle. But they fall into the "doing your part" category and do not have a large enough effect on the overall economy to stop the use of carbon fuels. As you develop a stronger commitment, think long term. The really big users of carbon are your electricity, your furnace, your car, your air travel, your purchases, your investments, and your diet. You might be able to change purchases and diet fairly quickly. Electricity, furnace, cars, and air travel will take longer. There's not a whole lot you can do about them right away. So don't worry about right away. Make the big changes when you make big changes in your life: when you buy a new car, buy or rent a new home, or change jobs. This is the time to boycott carbon.

Solar is a good example of a longer-range commitment. Do it when you can. But some very committed people will never be able to use solar panels on their houses. The thing I hate most about my job is telling people who really want to go solar that they don't have a suitable site and should not install panels. The other day I got an enthusiastic email from a potential client who wanted me to come over right away and tell her how much it would cost to make the move to renewable energy. She was ready. I looked up her address on satellite view and saw a nice, moderate-sized house with a large dormer and a skylight on the south-facing roof and a chimney that casts a shadow across the entire surface over the course of a day. There was barely enough room for three or four partially productive panels. Her electric usage, well over average, would require forty or fifty panels, in full sunlight. I've put off calling her, but I'm going to have to tell her it isn't worth it. Her site just isn't good enough. That happens a lot.

How do people like that make the transition to solar power? It's not as easy for them. They may have to wait until they move to another house. Or, they can take the group approach a step or two further, pushing for utility-provided green energy or community solar. Community solar is a group of neighbors getting together to find a site, perhaps a remote site, for a large enough solar array to provide electricity for several households. This can be done on a scale from three or four households to three or four hundred—or thousand. But community solar almost always involves a utility company. Electricity produced at the solar array is pumped into the nearest grid connection and used for general distribution by the utility, while credits are given to array owners to *offset* their household use. Each household purchases a given number of panels and receives credit for whatever they produce. It's a great idea, but the utility company has to go along with it, and many (most) utility companies want to maintain their monopoly of electrical production. Our own utility company in Louisville is an example. They're a good bunch of folks, but to keep multi-family electrical production in their own hands, they have introduced their own "community solar" program that is not community solar at all. They built a solar array, which is great, but they "sell" individual panels without actually transferring ownership. Then they charge a lot more than their normal rate for the electricity the panels you "bought" produce. What you end up with is a bigger electric bill and the right to *say* you use solar energy. Programs like this aim in the right general direction, but very few people are likely to be taken in by them. Community solar should mean community control.

One way or another, we are all going to have to stop using coal- and gas-fired electricity. Can we be committed and organized enough to stop using electricity altogether, until the power companies agree to buy wind power and build community solar arrays? That would be a hard way to go. We are so very dependent. Perhaps other tactics, or combinations of tactics, can be used instead of, or along with, reducing demand. Perhaps pressuring stockholders or public service commissions is the way to go.

Full-scale, rooftop, self-generated solar electricity may have to wait for trends in architecture and landscaping to catch up with the renewable energy revolution. Too often fancy gables, chimneys, or ornaments are plunked down in the middle of south-facing mounting surfaces, or roof vents and plumbing stacks shade or interrupt suitable surfaces. And then there are the ubiquitous poorly located trees. I love trees, but I hate it when their location prevents solar power from being a viable option. Plant them east, north, or west of the house, but not south! No need to cut down existing trees, but let's be more strategic about where we plant new trees. This, again, is a long-term adjustment. We may have to disregard existing homes with unsuitable rooftops and over look the trees blocking southern exposure. But let's build every new house with enough roof space for solar panels and plant every young tree with southern exposure in mind. To help create the impetus for needed changes, consider good solar exposure a priority when you are looking for a house, new or old. Whether you are talking to a real estate agent or an architect, help create the demand for renewable energy by investing in solar. The changes will take time. For decades into the future only some people—wealthier or middle-income people who happen to have a good roof—will have solar on their houses; the rest will have to depend on community solar or utility-scale solar installations. If you're stuck in a house unsuitable for solar, don't worry about it. Concentrate on making community solar happen on vacant lots, barn roofs, parking lots, and warehouses. You won't be able to do it overnight. Get started now, allow a few years, and get it right. Persistence is everything! Use your right as a consumer, a citizen, and a voter to demand clean energy. And do it with friends!

The commitment to boycott carbon may bring hardship, embarrassment, or financial difficulty at some point. It may be a challenge to finance a solar or a geothermal installation, and it may be hard to find an electric car that suits your needs. You may end up walking when you would rather ride. Your house may be too hot or too cold. Your commitment may embarrass your family and neighbors. You may end up eating a blander diet. Your clothes and furniture may be past their prime. This is where reinforcement from the group comes in. Rather than being embarrassed for not living up to the material standards you previously assumed, you will find that people in the group will accept and encourage your attempts to live up to your current values, values that include understanding what fossil fuels are doing to the Earth.

Try living more simply. A smaller house might do, or an older car. (Used electric cars are already on the market.) Eat less meat or no meat. Use less packaging. If you have a little space for a garden somewhere, try growing some food. That row of shell beans may come in handy someday. Don't grow food to save money—it's too much trouble for that. Do it to get your hands in the soil and see where life comes from. Do it to avoid tractors, trucks, and fertilizer factories.

Imagine yourself 10, 20, or 30 years from now. Where will you live? Who will you be with? What will be happening in the world? There is no way to know any of the particulars now. But the sooner you begin seeing your future self living in a responsible and practical manner, the easier it will be to do so. Do it in community with friends. And don't sweat the small stuff! Make the big moves when they come your way.

Alternative Energy Sources

A boycott never works without available alternatives. People will need another way to go, another thing to buy, another route around the object you are avoiding. If you boycott sugar, make sure honey is available. If you boycott Pepsi, be sure there is enough Dr. Pepper. Most people will not quit cold turkey; they want another way to achieve the same result. It's easier to redirect people than to stop them in their tracks.

The carbon boycott presents us with many potential alternatives: wind, solar, hydro, geothermal, biofuels, and all of the other energy sources humans have yet to discover. There are other sources of energy that can fuel most of the things we rely on fossil fuels for now; all we have to do is get people to start using them. Simple.

Wind

This is currently the biggest source of renewable energy. A recent study claimed that *all* the Earth's energy needs could be met with offshore wind turbines. You are most likely to see turbines now in rural areas, towering over cow pastures and cornfields, turning slowly in the breeze. (Actually, they're turning very fast; it only looks as if they are lumbering through each gigantic rotation because they are so big.) They make a lot of energy. I just heard that Texas now produces more energy from wind than from fossil fuel. Texas, of all places!

Wind is a wonderful source of energy on a large scale and works well in open, un-forested, or offshore regions. Trees and hills create drag that disturbs wind patterns. Wind energy is mostly available away from population centers, and the energy produced must be transmitted over long distances. Many people driving across the plains love to see wind turbines slowly spinning in the distance, but many of the same people would get tired of seeing them nearby every day. In some areas, there is strong resistance to new wind farms, especially offshore near wealthy coastal neighborhoods. And as mentioned earlier, wind turbines kill birds.

As far as individual access to wind energy is concerned, big turbines are expensive—in the million-dollar range—and you probably couldn't fit one in your back yard anyway. They also have moving parts—big ones—that require maintenance. A small turbine might work, but in most areas, you have to get it up pretty high above the trees to tap into consistent breezes. So, with some exceptions, you have to get wind energy through a utility company or a buying cooperative of some sort. You can lobby your local utility to buy wind power from adjoining areas. Because we are using more and more wind energy, the price is coming down.

SOLAR

The price is still coming down for solar, too. When I put solar on my house in 2007, I paid nearly a thousand dollars for each 200-watt panel. Today, a 385-watt panel costs under $200. Solar is still in its infancy. The panels we put up now are 20 percent efficient or less, which leaves a lot of room for improvement. As mentioned, there are trees, dormers, chimneys, vents, and zigzag rooflines that interfere with efficient installations. Rooflines do not need to be dull and boxy, but they should be designed with solar in mind—all of them! From now on, every new building in every corner of the world should be built with solar in mind! Capture that free energy! It's falling on your rooftop anyway. You can actually keep a building cooler by turning incoming photons into electrons. Very generally speaking, if properly designed (that is, with a few changes in architecture and landscaping and a little bit of engineering and investment), *every single-family house has enough roof space to produce all of its own energy and enough for an electric vehicle or two.* To repeat: every house can produce all the energy it needs! Commercial, industrial, municipal, and multi-family buildings may require more sun exposure than provided by their own rooftops, but well-designed single-family houses have enough. Moreover, solar can be installed on barns, warehouses, parking structures, and over vacant lots. Given time for innovation and creative new adaptations, solar can supply our energy needs.

Let us start building houses, roadways, parking areas, and public buildings for solar installation. Aim the ridgeline east-west instead of north-south (to create a southern roof exposure). Make the south side bigger than the north. Put the vents, antennas, chimneys, and plumbing stacks on the north side. Create an aggregate demand for appropriate architecture by insisting on good solar exposure. That starts today!

If you are fortunate enough to have good solar exposure already and wealthy enough to invest several thousand dollars into something that will not pay for itself for 12 years or so, go solar now. Money is not the main reason, but it is a good reason. A solar panel will likely last 30 to 50 years. (Actually, we don't know how long they will last—they have not been around that long.) Their performance degrades by about ½ percent per year, so they don't last forever. But they are all solid-state—no moving parts—so virtually maintenance-free. My installation crew has had a few panels broken in shipment and a few that did not work from the get-go, but we've never had to replace one once it was installed. The inverters (that change dc from the panels to the ac you use in your house) last around 20 years. So if you're a bean counter, expect a big investment upfront, a decade or more of payback period, and then several decades of free energy. You'll need a new inverter at some point for another thousand or two dollars. You'll be way ahead by then. Even if you borrow the money, your loan payments will be around what your electric bill is now. The solar on my house has already paid for itself, and I expect it to keep cranking out kilowatt-hours for the rest of my life. I don't buy electricity anymore.

But I tell potential customers that if saving money is the whole reason for installing solar, buy a savings bond instead. Solar is a good investment, but there are better ones if you're in it for the money. The real reason to go solar is that solar energy is how human civilization will survive on Earth.

I say this because solar is so primitive now. The panels we put up on rooftops are jalopies. They're Model Ts. They're like the old radios that took up half of the living room, or the computers that took up the entire basement of a university building. Panels are going to get more efficient, more compact, and more integrated into buildings and building materials. The whole idea of a *panel*, as a component separate from the building, may become obsolete. Better batteries will take the daytime and weather-related intermittency out of solar production. In time, solar energy will be collected in orbit. Earth-based solar is limited by clouds, nighttime, dust particles, and angles of incidence. Above the weather and beyond the shadow of the earth, a solar panel can be permanently aimed directly toward the sun 24 hours a day. Solar radiation above the atmosphere is already four times as intense. Here on Earth, solar panel installers are confronted with mounting surfaces that rotate with the day and change angles with the seasons. There are, of course, enormous technical difficulties in space-based solar collection, particularly in transmitting energy down to the ground, but if you're looking for where to go in the long term (and if you're reading this book, you are), solar is the direction to take. You won't even need batteries if you can get the panels out past the Earth's shadow!

HYDROPOWER

Hydroelectric is an excellent source of renewable electricity: no fuel, no pollution, no carbon, and around the clock service. But it's limited. There are only so many good locations for hydro, and most of them are taken. The age of dam building is over. Hydro production may increase marginally in the near future, but it is already reaching its limits.

Geothermal

Geothermal energy has a much more wide-open future. For individual buildings, five feet down is good enough to reach a year-round temperature of about 55 degrees Fahrenheit. My own house has two ¾" black plastic pipe loops containing a water/methanol mix in a single trench, three hundred feet long and five deep. The heat pump/air conditioner heats and cools from a 55-degree base instead of a 30, 90, or 0-degree base. It is extremely efficient, and the electricity it does use for the fan and compressor comes from the solar panels. I have talked to several people who have had mixed success with geothermal, but mine works great. My house is fairly small, well insulated, and I heat and cool only part of it. For free.

If you don't have 300' of space in your yard, you can also go straight down with a vertical geothermal heating/cooling system. It works about the same way, but there is more uncertainty in what you may end up drilling through.

Another long-range possibility is "deep geo": tapping into the natural nuclear heat of the Earth. Rock temperatures a thousand or so feet below the surface are measured in the hundreds of degrees. Developing piping and drilling equipment to withstand temperatures that high is a challenge, but the energy source is virtually limitless. Hot water pumped up from deep geothermal wells can be used to generate electricity or used directly to heat buildings. A large enough well could be used to heat an entire city.

Bio

Biofuel encompasses a large enough category to be extremely good and extremely bad at the same time. It's a carbon-based fuel but not *a fossil* fuel. The difference is that the carbon (ethanol, methane, even octane) comes from yesterday or last year, not a hundred million years ago. Biofuels take carbon *out* of the atmosphere when they are made, through photosynthesis. When they are burned a year or so later, the same carbon is released back into the atmosphere as carbon dioxide. Biofuels do not, therefore, increase the overall carbon dioxide content of the atmosphere and are *carbon net-zero*. When fossil fuels are burned, on the other hand, carbon dioxide that has been out of the atmosphere for hundreds of millions of years is released, increasing the atmosphere's overall carbon level. At the beginning of the aptly named *Carboniferous* period, 360 million years ago, the Earth's temperature was extremely hot: extremely high atmospheric CO_2, high sea levels, no ice caps, tropical forests up near the poles, etc. Then plants grew like crazy for 60 million years, sucking megatons of CO_2 out of the air through photosynthesis. As they died and were covered with earth and water over time, instead of their carbon going back into the air, enormous reservoirs of carbon were stored out of the air, underground, becoming coal, oil, and natural gas deposits. With less and less greenhouse gas in the air over the millennia, things cooled down. When people dig up and burn fossil fuels today, they are releasing stored carbon back into the air, restoring the hot, early carboniferous climate. Biofuels don't do that. They take carbon that is already in the air, store it temporarily as a fuel, and then release it. They're carbon neutral. That's the good part.

The bad part is that growing biofuels requires a lot of cropland and a lot of forestland. Crops such as corn that could feed people are processed instead to make ethanol fuel, which is mixed with gasoline. Many studies show that as much or more energy goes into tractor fuel and fertilizer to grow the corn as comes out of the finished product. A worse form of biofuel is derived from forest products. The original idea was to take "waste" products such as slabs, branches, sawdust, etc., and burn them to make electricity. But people in the business soon realized that they could use *living* "forest products" as well, like trees of any size. Whole forests have been clear-cut and processed to make "renewable" energy wood pellets. One pellet mill in North Carolina (Northampton) cuts down 18,000 acres of forestland every year. Technically the energy it produces is renewable; the problem is that the forest and all the living forms that depend on it will have a hard time renewing themselves for decades after so much energy, biomass, and nutrient matter is removed. This sort of biofuel is a sure recipe for biodegradation, deforestation, and ecological collapse. Crops such as switchgrass that do not require deforestation or annual replanting (permaculture crops), may have a better future.

An excellent possibility to replace *fossil* natural gas is *renewable* natural gas, from food waste, farm waste, and other biological sources. Methane (CH_4), the main ingredient of natural gas, is a product of anaerobic (oxygen-free) decomposition; piped to homes and factories and then oxidized in a furnace, it releases energy for space heating or other purposes. This technology is already in use, but whether it can be developed to a large enough scale to replace fossil methane is an open question.

Another great possibility for biofuel is algae. Without producing large, complex plant life, photosynthesis can be harnessed to turn sunlight into liquid fuel. We are going to need liquid fuel. We can use electricity for heating, cooling, cooking, communicating, and powering tractors, as well as for most forms of transportation, but there are a few things that will require onboard liquid fuel. Aircraft are an example, and perhaps ocean-going vessels and long-distance trucks and trains. Batteries are too heavy for planes (at least now) and too far from charging stations for ships and trains. Who knows what the future holds? But we are likely to need some form of liquid fuel for some things.

HYDROGEN

Another very good possibility for liquid fuel is hydrogen (a *fluid* fuel, if not liquid). Unlike solar, wind, or petroleum, hydrogen is not a *source* of energy. You have to make it from some other form of energy. Photosynthesis won't do it. The process is simple: run an electric current through water with an electrolyte (salt) added. The hydrogen part of the H_2O will split off from the oxygen. All you have to do is store the hydrogen gas somehow and burn (oxidize) it as a fuel when needed. Energy is released as oxygen reattaches to the hydrogen. The "exhaust," therefore, is H_2O: back to water. Very clean. But you need a source of energy, whether renewable or fossil, to produce the electric current in the first place. Solar, again, will do the job: you produce an electric current from a solar array, run it through water with an electrolyte, collect the hydrogen, store it in the airplane's fuel tank, and presto! You have a solar-powered airplane! The problem is, of course, the fuel tank. How do you store that much fuel in gaseous form? Or *do* you store it in gaseous form? People are working on it. Air travel is going to be a concern for the carbon boycott. I have kids on the other side of the continent. At what point do we (I) refuse to fly until airplanes use renewable energy? There's a topic for the next group meeting.

*   *   *

If we had to stop using fossil fuels tomorrow morning, we could not do it. There's not enough wind power, solar is too primitive, hydro is too small, and deep geothermal is still a fringe technology. There's just not enough renewable energy available now to do what we think we have to do. There's not enough "to meet demand," as they say. But what is *demand*? Demand is us, buying stuff. Demand is consumers investing in alternative energy. The economy is designed to accommodate demand.

Demand is not a given. Demand is created by the consumer.

A boycott is the conscious creation of alternative demand.

To boycott carbon, we need not

> defeat anyone
> declare anyone evil, or
> convince the inconvincible.

We need only to stop buying it.

Meanwhile: August 15, 2019

NOAA, the National Oceanic and Atmospheric Administration, confirmed today that last month, July 2019, was the hottest July since record-keeping began and that the all-time hottest June on record was the previous month: June of 2019.

100% REAL Update: August 16, 2019

Kentucky Attorney General Andy Beshear (also a Democratic candidate for governor) has intervened on the side of Bernheim Forest against the proposed gas pipeline. This will at least delay the project.

5

Tea, Salt, Buses, and Apartheid

Boycotts in the future will be like boycotts in the past—and different. This chapter looks at four examples of previous attempts to enact change through such methods. The tea boycott and the Boston Tea Party, Gandhi's Salt March, the Montgomery Bus Boycott, and the dismantling of apartheid in South Africa.

Tea

The American federal union began as a boycott society.

The Stamp Act of 1765 was consummately logical. The British government had exhausted its treasury defending the American colonies from Indians and the French. The colonies should help pay for their own defense. Right? Why not a small tax on everyday items? If Britain could send thousands of young men across the water to fight for English people in America, why not send a few pounds back the other way in appreciation? Were we not all one big family? What would have happened to the American colonies if Britain had not defended them?

This, of course, was the logic from the British point of view. All English were English, and all should chip in. The center of the English world was, of course, England. Everything radiated from that center. The mercantilist philosophy of the times assumed that the purpose of settling and defending overseas colonies was to enhance the economic and military power of the mother country in its continuing struggle with other imperial powers. What surprised the British, and the Americans, was that a new center was coming into being beneath the surface. Few realized on a conscious level that the American people no longer saw themselves as subordinate colonists. They were still English—and demanded their rights as English—but the American English were beginning to look at the world from the perspective afforded by their distinct geography.

Deep within their collective psyche, Americans were becoming a separate people and beginning to create a separate axis of collective behavior. The separation came to the surface in the form of taxes.

From the American point of view, the Stamp Tax was an outrage. The British Parliament assumed the right to place taxes on paper documents of all kinds, collect the revenue, and bring it back to Britain. But the assumed right provoked riots and mob violence in the streets of Boston, New York, Philadelphia, and Charleston. Officials appointed to collect the tax were hanged in effigy and threatened with physical harm until they resigned their posts. Their houses were looted and vandalized, their furniture dragged into the streets and burned. An adolescent society was asserting its right to self-identity, while the mother country needed funds to keep the family together. The financial problem could have been solved in any number of ways; both sides could have saved thousands of lives and millions of pounds. The war cost many times more than the taxes would have yielded. Trade across the Atlantic was brisk and lucrative; the money could have been found somewhere, one way or the other. Peace would have been cheaper. From a purely fiscal point of view, the American Revolutionary War need not have happened.

But the uproar in the colonies was not over taxes or the money they would have raised; the uproar was over the right to tax. The reaction in the colonies to the Stamp Act (besides the violence in the streets) was the formation of a Stamp Act Congress. Representatives from each of the 13 colonies were invited to meet in New York in October of 1765 to discuss what to do and how to do it (just before the Stamp taxes were to go into effect on November 1). Delegates from 9 colonies showed up. After three weeks of discussion, the congress acted politically and economically. It issued a 14-part Declaration of Rights and Grievances listing taxes and other rights violations imposed without representation on the American people, and sent a copy across the ocean to Parliament. The congress went on from there to organize a "continental" boycott. The boycott worked—the Stamp Act was repealed by Parliament the following year.

Before the Stamp Act Congress, American political or economic organization barely existed on the "continental" level. Each colony had a direct relation to the mother country and virtually no relation to other colonies. There was a coastal trade up and down the Atlantic seaboard, but transatlantic trade was far more significant. People in New York knew more about what was happening in London or Liverpool than about the goings-on in Philadelphia or Charleston. The Stamp Act Congress was the first attempt to begin direct communications among the various colonies and to organize them as a united front. It was necessary to speak to Parliament with one voice in responding to the Stamp Act, but it was even more necessary to act as one body in declaring and enforcing the boycott. If one or two colonies continued to import from (and export to) Britain, the boycott would weaken and fail.

The day before the Stamp Act went into effect, over 700 merchants from New York, Boston, and Philadelphia agreed to stop importing all but a few British goods, beginning the next morning. The boycotted goods included mostly luxury items: gloves, hats, lace, furniture, clocks, glue, mustard, cheese, and tea. Within two months, British imports had dropped by 14 percent and were dropping further. Merchants in Britain with warehouses full of unsold goods began urging Parliament to repeal the Stamp Act. George Washington quipped, "I fancy the merchants of Great Britain trading to the colonies will not be among the last to wish for a repeal of it."

There was sympathy in London for the American cause. In a speech to Parliament William Pitt, the former prime minister, stated, "The Americans are the sons of, and not the bastards of, England.... I will be held to affirm, that the profits to Great Britain from the trade of the colonies, through all its branches, is two million (pounds) a year. This is the fund that carried you triumphantly through the last war.... (Let) the Stamp Act be repealed absolutely, totally, and immediately ... because it was founded on an erroneous principle." Nevertheless, Pitt concluded with an assertion that Parliament retained the right to govern the colonies in "every point of legislation whatsoever."

The financial pinch of the boycott embodied in the appeals of the British merchant class led directly to the repeal of the Stamp Act, while the list of political grievances was repudiated or ignored. And so ended the first crisis of the American Revolution.

During the 1760s and 70s, the British attempted to establish political and economic control over the colonies three times and were forced to retreat three times. The first wave was the just-described Stamp Act of 1765, repealed in 1766. Pressured by members of its own merchant class, many of whom held seats in Parliament, the British government was forced to backtrack on a policy it felt it had the right to pursue. But as Pitt suggested in his speech, Parliament retained the right to tax in the so-called Declaratory Act issued when the Stamp Act was withdrawn. Parliament was backing off a policy, but not surrendering a right. The second wave was parallel to the first: a new series of taxes on the colonies, known as the Townsend Acts, was passed by Parliament in 1767. These were taxes on consumer items: glass, paper, lead, paint, and tea. Again, the colonies revolted, new boycotts were declared, British merchants lost money, and the taxes had to be repealed. Again, to assert its right to tax the colonies, parliament withdrew the Townsend taxes except for the tax on tea. This had great consequences for the overall course of the American Revolution. The third wave, precipitated by the tax on tea, lead to renewed boycotts and the Boston Tea Party, which was answered in a series of Parliamentary acts closing the port of Boston. Parliament did not back down this time until after the battle of Yorktown nine years later. By then, the underlying meaning of the American Revolution had come to the surface.

With the issue of the Townsend Acts, a boycott on British goods began anew. A Boston town meeting on October 28, 1767, passed and approved a list of British goods to be boycotted. Copies of the list were sent to other New England towns and some other colonies. Soon stronger measures were taken by Boston merchants for a total boycott: "...we will not import on our own account, or on commissions, or

Purchase from any who shall import from any other colony in America from January 1, 1769, to January 1, 1770, any tea, glass, paper, or other goods commonly imported from Great Britain … until the Acts imposing duties on these articles have been repealed." Merchants in Salem soon joined in, then merchants in New York and Virginia. The New York boycott also included shops selling British goods at retail. John Hancock of Massachusetts urged a partial boycott, asking colonists to make their own clothing, cordage, and cheeses. Churches in New England responded by organizing women's spinning circles to reduce dependence on British imports. Twenty-eight towns in Massachusetts formed spinning bees. But New Hampshire and New Jersey did not participate in the boycott after the Townsend Acts; and Loyalist merchants in Boston, New York, and other colonies refused to go along. (Some pointed out the irony of colonial patriots protesting for their liberty while imposing coercive measures on others.) By 1769 Hancock began urging a full boycott that eventually reduced British colonial imports by 38 percent.

(Note: The colonists used the word non-importation. The term boycott is traceable to the 1890s when Irish tenants refused to pay rents to their landlord, Charles Cunningham Boycott, until grievances were satisfied.)

When British troops were sent to Boston to "protect" the colony, the local population viewed them as occupiers sent to enforce illegal measures. Tensions between citizens and soldiers mounted, and street fights broke out across the city leading to the Boston Massacre of 1770.

Organized groups of New Englanders wrote up lists of merchants refusing to honor the boycott on tea and ostracized them publicly. Other colonists wore homespun clothing to demonstrate their independence from British luxuries. Students at Harvard announced they would drink no more tea. Women, who shouldered much of the willpower behind the boycott, developed a sense of political conscience and participation as a result. Men and women, rich and poor, master and servant, all felt a common sense of participation in the fate of their country as they denied themselves the simple pleasure of a cup of hot tea in the afternoon.

The Carbon Boycott

The Townsend Acts were repealed later in 1770, due less to the protests of the colonials than to the protests of British merchants suffering from the boycott. Action in colonial meeting houses and in the streets calmed down during the so-called "pause in politics" between 1770 and 1773. The boycott began to waver. Non-importation caused shortages and drove up prices. Support among merchants slacked off. New York merchants began importing again despite continued pressure from Boston to continue the boycott. Supporters of the crown had reason to believe that colonists would soon forget the boycott and resume their role as loyal consumers and royal subjects. The "pause" ended with the Tea Act of 1773.

Americans were consuming over a million pounds of tea a year before the boycott began. But as a result of the boycott and other troubles in Bengal, the British East India Company was nearing bankruptcy in 1773. Lord North, Prime Minister of Britain, had a bright idea: there might be a way to bail out the "too big to fail" East India Company and at the same time force the colonies to submit to paying taxes. Parliament would repeal the tax on tea, but give the East India Company a monopoly on the tea trade, and allow it to collect a lower tax, which it could keep for itself. The price of tea would decline substantially as a result, becoming cheaper than smuggled Dutch tea. With cheaper tea, Americans would abandon their boycotts and moralistic abstentions, forget their sense of patriotism, relax, have a cup of tea, and fall into line. With the right to tax thus established, any number of other taxes could be imposed and the treasury filled. North was certain the Americans would cave in. "Men will always go to the cheapest markets," he quipped. This was the Tea Act. King George loved the idea: the boycott would end and he would have renewed sway over the empire.

But tea boycotters were more committed and more organized than ever. They turned to substitutes, including raspberry leaves, Labrador tea, and redroot bush. The resulting brews were barely palatable. But many insisted on drinking them purely for the sake of defiance. Rumors spread among boycotters that British tea caused all manner of ill health. Some Bostonians even tried to grow Chinese tea bushes; but Boston, it turns out, is not China.

The boycott on consumption required sacrifice on the part of many caffeine-addicted patriots. Tea drinking was an ingrained American habit. A New York merchant noted that tea is used in America "by people of all denominations, from the Gentlemen even to the Slave; and is so much in Vogue, that the most menial Servant will not be Satisfied without it." Tea was healthier than un-boiled drinking water, and of great social value, particularly among women. It brightened eyes in the morning and enlivened conversation in the afternoon. Kicking the tea habit would not be easy. Tea continued to be imported by Loyalist merchants, often in chests labeled otherwise, or mixed in with other items. But patriotic ladies continued to honor the boycott, as expressed in these verses from A Lady's Adieu to her Tea Table:

> No more shall my teapot so generous be
> In filling the cups with this pernicious tea,
> For I'll fill it with water and drink out the same,
> Before I'll lose LIBERTY that dearest name.
> Because I am taught (and believe it is fact)
> That our ruin is aimed in the late act,
> Of imposing a duty on all foreign Teas,
> Which detestable stuff we can quit when we please.

With the repeal of the Townsend taxes except for tea, tea became the focal point for the conflict over the right to tax. Taxation is, of course, the right of any sovereign body. For both Britain and America, tea thereby became a symbol in the struggle for national identity. The Tea Act would prove to be the turning point. If Lord North and King George were right—if economic forces were stronger than patriotism—cheaper prices would lead Americans to buy the tea, dissolve the boycott, and resume their subordinate status in the imperial system as British subjects. If Sam Adams, John Hancock, and Paul Revere were right—if people were able to see beyond their economic appetite—they would refuse the tea, defend their rights, and become a separate people as events proceeded.

In October of 1773, seven East India Company ships sailed for America laden with two thousand chests of tea. If they wouldn't take the tea voluntarily, Parliament was going to shove it down their throats. One ship sailed for Philadelphia, one for New York, one for Charleston, and four for Boston. Citizens in Philadelphia, mostly Sons of Liberty, met the ship at the dock and threatened the consignees (who were chosen to sell the tea) into resigning their positions. They suggested to the ship's captain that he could avoid tarring and feathering were he to turn the ship around without unloading the tea. He obliged and the ship headed back across the ocean. In Charleston, the local Sons of Liberty also convinced tea consignees to resign their positions. This time the tea was unloaded, but locked in storage. No duty was ever paid. In New York, the Sons of Liberty made enough of a presence on the dock to convince the ship's captain to return across the ocean with all tea still aboard.

Things did not go so smoothly in Boston. Three of the four ships arrived at Griffin's Wharf and waited, tea on board, while the town decided what to do. Boston had been the center of anti–British activity since the days of the Stamp Act, but the tea boycott was not as effective there as in New York and Philadelphia. The Sons of Liberty, who were under pressure from colleagues in other colonial cities to do something decisive with the tea, ruled the streets and the meetinghouses of Boston. But the colonial governor, loyal to the British throne, had the royal navy ready to block the retreat of the ships from Boston Harbor. The ships could not leave the harbor and had to be unloaded, one way or another. Showdown time!

Over 5000 people (about a third of the population) turned out at a Boston Town Meeting a few blocks from the Wharf to determine what was to be done. One of the ship owners explained his predicament to the crowd and then, while the crowd waited, walked to the governor's mansion to plead for his ship's safe passage out of the harbor, tea, and all. The governor refused permission. There was nothing left for the meeting to do, and a sense of desperation weighed on the crowd. But as darkness descended, a strange hooting and hollering was heard on the street outside the meeting room. Men dressed up as Mohawk Indians, their faces darkened with coal ash and bodies colored with war paint, filed into the meeting. Confusion ruled in the crowd. Who were these people? Was this some sort of plan? Back on the street outside, the "Mohawks" marched toward the wharf, torches ablaze. The crowd followed. What were these guys up to?

The "Mohawks" split up and boarded each of the three ships. Seizing control from the crew, they lugged tea chests from the hold up on deck, smashed the chests open, and dumped the tea into the harbor.

This little piece of street theater ignited the American Revolution.

I say street theater because it was, in fact, theater. Having heard the story many times, I always envisioned the "Mohawks" sneaking on the vessels in the middle of the night when nobody was watching. But in reality, everybody was watching. Everybody. Thousands thronged the streets: the crowd from the meeting, ship owners and ship captains, deckhands, constables, women, children, dogs and cats—even the military was watching from a fort across the harbor—a vantage point from which they would not fire on the crowd. Torches glowed everywhere, lighting the stage. The actors were so confident, the plan so audacious, the crowd so supportive, the general population so annoyed, and the authorities were so taken aback by the drama of the moment that there was nothing anybody could do or would do, to stop the action.

But why the dress up? Everybody knew these "Mohawks" were not real Indians. Partly, they dressed up to disguise their identities—to give fellow Bostonians a sense of deniability—but mostly they did it to create a heightened sense of counter reality. This was theater. This was not a normal moment. This was not a normal action. This was a showdown. Actors in costume drew the audience away from the mundane reality of everyday life and delivered them to an otherworldly sense of history in the making. This little piece of history was going to be remembered. What would we remember of it now had it not been theater?

And it was well-rehearsed theater. Nobody knows for sure who came up with the idea, developed the cast, and directed the stage. (Sam Adams had to be in on it one way or another.) Everyone in the cast was sworn to secrecy, though the word got out over the years. The actors were coopers, rope makers, farmers, merchants, cabinet makers, painters, upholsterers, coach makers, carpenters, masons, mariners, sailors, distillers, innkeepers, booksellers, horse traders, hatters, printers, shoemakers, caulkers, teamsters, clerks, apprentices, barbers, blacksmiths, dockworkers, schoolteachers, engravers, silversmiths, laborers, bricklayers, ship joiners, cordwainers, fishermen, and a physician: a hundred men or so in all. Some in heavy disguise, some with but a feather or a stripe of face paint, others with no costume at all. Each knew his part.

As they reached the wharf they divided into three groups, one for each ship. Men stood sentry on the dock and at the bow of each ship. Other men boarded, demanded keys to the hatchways, and access to hoisting tackle and ropes. On one ship the captain and crew were detained below deck, after assurances they would remain unharmed. Several customs officials were escorted off the ships and watched the drama unfold with the rest of the crowd. All the participants were carefully disciplined; they were instructed to avoid violent confrontation and to respect the ship and any of the ship's cargo that was not tea.

Lifting, uncrating, and dumping 46 tons of tea is not easy work, even for a hundred men. They toiled quietly for two or three hours, careful to avoid unnecessary damage to the ships' equipment. This was a port city and these were men who knew boats. Those who knew how to get to the cargo and how to use hoisting tackle brought the tea chests up to the deck from the hold. Others broke the chests open with axes. Still others threw the tealeaves and broken chests over the rail. There was so much tea, and the tide so low, that mounds of tealeaves piled up above the water level. Men waded out in the shallows and broke up the mounds as best they could, but the bulk of the tea leaves did not drift out of the harbor until high tide the next morning. When they had completed their task, the men carefully swept the decks clean. A broken padlock was later replaced. By 8 or 9 p.m., $2.2 million worth of cargo had been destroyed, and the tea party was over. The "Mohawks" lined up on the dock and marched off in military fashion.

I wasn't there, but I imagine the crowd roared in approval.

We're still roaring.

Parliament immediately responded from across the ocean—as immediately as one could in the eighteenth century—with what they called the Coercive Acts, shutting down Boston Harbor and suspending the Massachusetts charter, the constitutional basis of colonial government. Local elections, town meetings, and jury trials were suspended until the citizens of Boston paid for the destroyed cargo. This same series of laws became known in America as the Intolerable Acts. The British had hoped to isolate Massachusetts from the other colonies by cracking down hard and making an example. The opposite happened. Each of the other colonies realized the same could happen to them. The result was a quantum leap of organized support throughout America.

Even before the Stamp Act, activists in Boston and New York had formed what they called committees of correspondence—groups of letter writers specifically authorized to keep in contact with other such groups, originally in other cities and villages in their own colony. The idea spread. Virginia later suggested that every colony form such a committee and begin corresponding with every other colony. The result was something of a shadow government that could plan actions and coordinate strategy against the British. The committees of correspondence were the reason Sons of Liberty chapters formed in Philadelphia, Charleston, and New York as well as in Boston, and the committees of correspondence were the reason coordinated resistance to the tea shipments became possible. But the committees were inter-colonial, not supra-colonial: there was no authority on the "continental" level. The impetus to extend the idea of the centralized Stamp Act Congress of 1765 did not re-emerge until after the Tea Party of 1773. New York suggested that a convention of representatives from all colonies, or a Continental Congress, be instituted to discuss what to do next. Should the colonies renew a boycott on all British imports and exports? Pennsylvania, Maryland, Connecticut, New Hampshire, New Jersey, Virginia, and South Carolina all agreed to send delegates.

Delegates from twelve colonies came to the First Continental Congress of 1774. Radical separatists generally outnumbered

Conservative loyalists, but the idea of independence was not discussed openly. There was an undertone of complete separation among some in attendance (particularly in private sessions), but collectively the King was still affirmed as sovereign. The Americans would still be English Americans, but the Intolerable Acts were specifically rejected. Massachusetts should be allowed its own laws, taxes, and militia.

A Continental Association was formed to monitor and enforce the boycott on British goods. Interestingly, the association called not only for non-importation but non-consumption of tea. Virginia worried about selling its tobacco crop, and South Carolina worried about selling its rice crop. But the principle of cutting off all economic ties generally prevailed.

A great feeling of unity prevailed throughout the sessions, and the Congress agreed to meet again in May 1775. All colonies approved terms proclaimed by the Continental Association, and despite failures to comply in some cases the boycott became a great success. Imports to Maryland and Virginia were reduced from 690,000 pounds in 1774 to 2000 pounds in 1775. Tea protests continued outside of Massachusetts and public tea burnings took place in New Hampshire, New York, New Jersey, and Rhode Island. A shipload of tea was thrown overboard in Virginia, openly endorsing the actions taken in Boston. All along the Atlantic seaboard from Portsmouth to Charleston, Americans came to see tea as a sign of British oppression and stood firm behind the patriots in Boston.

In January 1775 hundreds of British merchants met in London to again petition Parliament, asking for the repeal of any legislation causing the boycott. They claimed that the Stamp Act, Townsend Acts, and Tea Act harmed not only merchants, but artisans, manufacturers, and public revenue. This time, Parliament ignored the petitioners. Things had gone too far in Boston.

As the First Continental Congress disbanded, a ship in Annapolis, Maryland, with 2000 pounds of tea was burned to the waterline, tea, and all. In 1775, as representatives were busy planning the Second Continental Congress, patriots and redcoats in Lexington and Concord fired the shots heard round the world. A man with a musket could no longer be both English and American. It was time to take sides, once and for all.

The Second Continental Congress continued the boycott, gathered arms, appointed a general, began training troops, and a year later, commissioned a document explaining the meaning and purpose of Independence.

In this instance, boycotts were the right answer to the wrong question. However hard they may have been to promulgate and enforce, the boycotts got the British to back down every time. They worked. Lord North was wrong: people do not always go to the cheapest markets. Americans were able to see beyond their immediate consumer needs to the higher, albeit abstract, goals of liberty and justice. They organized, developed alternatives (such as they were), and committed their behavior to a higher cause. They learned to think and act with their intellect and values and not just with their pockets. More importantly, through the Stamp Act Congress, the Committees of Correspondence, and the Continental Congresses they learned to organize on the supra-colonial, "continental" level. Through organized non-importation, Americans began the evolutionary process that would develop into the United States federal government.

But the real problem—the problem the boycotts brought to the surface—was much deeper. Had the issue really been taxes, the boycotts of the 1760s and 70s would have addressed the problem, and the British Empire would have continued as before, with improved systems of tax administration.

The American boycotts of the eighteenth century utilized one effective tool that boycotts of the twenty-first century can't wield —violence. Not armed violence for the most part, but violence— roughing up, breaking windows, vandalizing houses, intimidating merchants and consumers of boycotted goods, and intimidating families of merchants and consumers. Honoring the boycotts was not always a matter of personal choice, and didn't have to be. The most effective way to assure adherence to a boycott was the threat of the mob. If the mob found out your wife bought a pound of tea...

The Sons of Liberty were a long way from being terrorists in the modern sense, but their intimidating tactics were persuasive. We may not associate ourselves with such behavior, but we should know that the boycotts of the time would not have worked without it.

A more serious form of violence broke out in response to the real issue of the American Revolution: the separation of one people from another. To become psychically American and not English, patriots had to fight physically against the English. They had to experience the fear of the other side aiming muskets at them, ready to shoot. Each man and woman had to pass close enough to death to re-emerge in life as a new kind of person. The dividing lines that had formed during street fights and shootings in Boston deepened at Lexington and Concord and ruptured into murderous violence at the outbreak of the War. To this day, with very few exceptions, we still don't know how to do revolutionary change any other way. We will learn, but we have not yet learned. We have learned to do boycotts without violence, but not how to create two political sovereignties from one, or one from two, without violence. We have not yet found reliable ways to make sovereign political change without hurting people.

Fortunately, sovereign political change and hurting people are not called for in the current struggle against fossil fuel; we don't have to divide; we don't want to divide. This time we have to stay united— not united in opposition—united. In today's struggle, there are no good guys and bad guys, no patriots and redcoats. There is only one atmosphere and everyone is in it together. Without a common enemy to unite us we must reveal peacefully that which is true: that which would reveal itself in time if there were enough time. We have to bring truth to the surface with a new kind of boycott that does not use intimidation. We don't have to scare anyone. Were we to use the mob to discipline non-compliers, we would find the mob as likely to be against as for us. This boycott will be peaceful: no intimidation. No matter how physically patriotic some of us might have been in Boston 250 years ago, we now must be committed and organized without violence or the threat of violence.

Boycotts can be purely passive. Just don't buy it, whatever it is. Just stay away from tea. But the carbon boycott will not be passive.

Peaceful, but not passive. Commitment and organization will be more important than ever. More important still will be promoting and choosing alternative sources of energy. Whereas in 1773 a few boycott zealots might have been satisfied with red root bush alternative at tea-time, today we have to demonstrate that there are other ways to fuel our 21st-century lives.

Meanwhile: August 23, 2019

The Amazon is burning. Tens of thousands of fires are raging through the largest tropical forest on Earth. Most are purposely set by farmers and ranchers clearing land to increase production. Brazil's president Bolsonaro, the "Trump of the Tropics," who has been encouraging the economic development of the rain forest, blamed the fires on environmentalists. But he admits that the fires are out of control and impossible for Brazil alone to manage. President Macron of France said today, "Our house is on fire."

Salt

Mohandas Gandhi was the ideal spiritual and political leader of the Indian independence movement and the perfect embodiment of austerity, simple living, and other-worldly self-control. But the ideal and the perfect rarely mix with the real and the practical. Much of what Gandhi envisioned never took place in the real world. He was right—always right—but the ethereal truth he embodied spread and thinned before it reached the ground. That is why he was a great soul—a Maha Atma. He did not fully live in this world. He did not get his signals from the opinions and conformities of other people. Those around him wore suits and ties; he wore homespun fabric. Modern factories throughout India churned out miles of machine cloth; he worked the spinning wheel. Outcaste untouchables were denied entrance to public schools and temples; he spoke of human equality in absolute terms. Violence ruled the streets on every side; he preached non-violence.

Gandhi's great achievement was in defining a new Indian identity vis-à-vis the British Empire, an identity that honored the opponent and allowed political separation of Britain and India largely free of overt violence. His great failure was in not establishing an Indian identity vis-à-vis the Indian people themselves. Muslims and Hindus never came to see each other, or themselves, as national Indians. They could be loyal subjects, together, of the British Empire, but free of the British, they could not be Indian together. We can hardly blame Gandhi for this "failure," yet Gandhi blamed himself. The world he lived in saw no distinction between Hindu and Muslim, Brahman or Dalit, and the world he lived in hated the hatred and violence between them. But he could not bring the world he lived into the world everyone else lived in, the world we would call the real world. Despite Gandhi's constant pleading, the political separation between Muslim and Hindu was one of the most violent in history.

But what interests us here is Gandhi's use of the boycott. In India, as in America, the boycott of British goods and institutions was a tool from the beginning of the independence movement. Under Gandhi's leadership, the great "non-cooperation" or Satyagraha movement for swaraj (self-rule) took place in three waves: in the early 1920s, the early 30s, and the mid-40s. Gandhi called a halt to the first two waves in 1922 and 34 as they degenerated into violence. In 1942 the entire Indian National Congress leadership including Gandhi was arrested as a wartime measure.

Born in India in 1869, Mohandas Gandhi received his higher education in Britain and spent twenty years of his early adult life in South Africa as a lawyer and social activist. When he returned to India in 1915 at age 45, he was well known by his countrymen for the successful non-violent movement he led for the rights of South African Indians, both Hindu and Muslim. Advised by his mentor to spend his first year back getting to know the country while refraining from speaking out against British Imperial rule, Gandhi spent his time traveling through large cities, small towns, and rural villages in the land of his birth. The vast majority of Indians lived in small agricultural villages without plumbing, electricity, transportation, or other modern conveniences. Large crowds greeted him wherever he went. These were the people Gandhi wanted to know more intimately—the people who looked up to him politically and spiritually for the next thirty years of his life.

Before the coming of the British, hand spinning and weaving of cotton clothing were widespread in India, providing clothing and employment for millions of the rural poor, especially in the agricultural off-season. This all changed with the importation of foreign machinery and the machine production of cloth, which ruined the local economies of nearly every village in the land and destroyed the Indian sense of self-worth. "Love of foreign cloth has brought foreign domination, pauperism, and what is worse, shame to many a home," Gandhi observed. It put many poor people, especially women, out of work. After food, clothing is the most basic of human needs. Why should India depend on foreign traders, factories, and machinery? Why not produce its own yarn and woven cloth by employing its own people locally, instead of forcing them off the land to seek employment in large cities? Why not keep the money for clothing in the countryside, rather than sending it off to England?

In the summer of 1919, Gandhi initiated a program at his ashram in Gujarat to encourage hand spinning and weaving of khadi, or homespun clothing. Ashram members were required to sit at the wheel and spin every day, and to produce a minimum quantity of yarn. For the country as a whole, Gandhi told a reporter, "I want every man, woman, and child to learn hand-spinning and weaving." He told his Muslim colleague, Muhammad Ali Jinnah, that he expected his (Jinnah's) wife to learn to spin. Gandhi even went so far as to offer spinning lessons to the wife of the British governor of Bombay!

The other side of encouraging local self-sufficiency was, of course, discouraging the purchase of foreign clothing. Boycotting was a long-standing tradition in village India before Gandhi came along, but had never been attempted on a national level. In village

India, economic function was divided along caste lines: the butcher, the baker, and the candlestick maker were each born into their profession and blood-related primarily to people within their caste. In such a tight-knit community, inter-caste issues were often addressed through informal boycotts: if you don't like the way shoes are being made, get the whole caste to stop buying them. If your caste is not performing up to standard, expect the other castes to let you know about it in an organized manner. Word of mouth communication and peer pressure were direct and effective on the village level but non-existent on the national level. Gandhi's attempt to establish a boycott for all of India would effectively create a national level.

In addition to manufactured British clothing, the boycott covered foreign luxuries in general, including French and Japanese silks. Classes in hand spinning and weaving were taught and encouraged throughout the country. Everyone in every walk of life was asked, and often pressured, to spend some time each day at the spinning wheel. Some high society ladies joined the khadi movement, spinning and sewing publicly in support of the boycott and popularizing domestically produced patriotic clothing by wearing khadi, no matter how rustic it might appear to the fashion-conscious. At first, as he was not yet advocating a complete break from the British Empire, Gandhi opposed the public burning of factory-produced clothing. However, he soon changed his position, sanctioning the practice and even lighting fires himself. Burning foreign cloth was a more aggressive and more effective way of supporting the boycott than the purely passive practice of not buying. "We are purifying ourselves by discarding foreign cloth which is the badge of our slavery."

Both men and women took an active part in the khadi movement, but women were discouraged from the more openly active practices in what Gandhi called a "man's fight." Nevertheless, many women were already supporting the boycott on their own initiative by spinning and weaving at home and by picketing liquor stores in public. Gandhi encouraged them, and excise revenues on alcoholic beverages declined in Punjab, Bihar, Orissa, and Bombay.

At the India National Congress meeting in Calcutta in 1920,

Gandhi announced a seven-point program of Satyagraha, (or truth force) against British rule. Indian nationals were asked to:

- Surrender titles and honorary posts
- Refuse to attend government functions
- Gradually withdraw children from government schools
- Establish national schools to replace them
- Gradually boycott British courts (by lawyers and litigants)
- Refuse to serve overseas as soldiers, laborers, or clerks
- Boycott foreign goods

To bring the boycott to the local level, Gandhi drew up a plan to send volunteers " from door to door in every village" to collect foreign cloth to be "publicly burnt." Also, "picketing foreign cloth shops may be undertaken wherever possible.... Help of patriotic ladies should be enlisted.... A small Foreign Cloth Boycott Committee should be formed...." In Calcutta, he told a crowd he wanted them to burn foreign cloth "as you burn rags ... even as a drunkard suddenly becomes a teetotaller empties his cupboard and destroys every bottle of brandy and whiskey.... You will count no cost too great against the ... liberty and honour of your country."

Gandhi rashly stated to the congress that if his program were followed to the letter, without violence, swaraj (self-rule) would be attained within a single year. The measure passed easily, but so did the year. Results took longer than expected, but by 1921 the boycotts and other forms of non-cooperation were taking effect and the government was forced to respond with renewed repression. Thousands of activists were arrested. Satyagrahis in Bengal, Madras, Bombay, Sindh, and Calcutta were arrested at meetings, in picket lines at liquor stores, and at cloth burning demonstrations. Others were arrested for possessing forbidden literature in their homes and on the streets. Gandhi answered with another round of stricter Satyagraha, this time including non-payment of land taxes. Tensions heightened; the boycotts were clearly disrupting British rule, but crowds were becoming increasingly unruly. Over and over again Gandhi insisted on strict adherence to non-violence. The means were more important than the end. But at a demonstration at Chauri Chaura, a provoked crowd turned violent against the police, burning down the police station, killing 23 policemen. Gandhi immediately suspended the movement, calling off all forms of civil disobedience, and began a personal five-day fast in penance for the lives lost.

Other national leaders criticized Gandhi for sacrificing the momentum of the independence movement for a single incident of violence, but Gandhi would not be moved. At his word the Satyagraha of the early 1920s came to a sudden end. But many had grown weary of Gandhi's unending demands for spinning and the wearing of khadi. Boycotts and protests were dwindling, and the movement was running out of steam. The 1926 All India Spinners Association reported that there were 42,959 hand spinners in India—a large number for the organization, but a small number for a country of 319,000,000. One young nationalist leader by the name of Jawaharlal Nehru wrote to Gandhi: "It was difficult to believe it (self-rule as a result of spinning and wearing khadi) would happen, but faith in your amazing capacity to bring off the impossible kept us in an expectant mood. But such faith for an irreligious person like me is a poor reed to rely on and I am beginning to think if we are to wait for freedom until khadi becomes universal in India, we shall have to wait until the Greek Kalends." Meanwhile, riots and killings mounted between police and Indians, and increasingly, between Hindus and Muslims.

At the Congress meeting in 1928, Motilal Nehru (Jawaharlal's father) proposed that nationalists request dominion status within the British Commonwealth for India, with a deadline of one year (i.e., by December 31, 1929). If Britain refused the request, Congress would demand full independence and organize a renewed Satyagraha: a non-violent, nation-wide program of non-cooperation including a boycott of councils and legislatures, a boycott of all British goods and institutions, and non-payment of taxes.

When the British government failed to grant dominion status by the end of 1929, the push for full independence began. Voices for armed rebellion were growing louder, and Gandhi thought hard about what to do next. In January he wrote to Jawaharlal Nehru, "Ever since we have separated at Lahore, I have been evolving schemes of civil disobedience. I have not seen my way clear as yet." This is a problem every non-violent movement faces—what to be non-violent about. Non-violence is a negative—it's all about not doing something. But what do you do when you're making a point of not doing? Passive resistance, of course! Don't obey the laws! Don't buy the goods! Don't pay the taxes! Boycotts are a great tool for non-violence because you don't have to do anything, but boycotts do not always catch the public imagination the way a good demonstration can—especially a violent demonstration or a fully-armed rebellion. People pay attention to violence. Violence is wonderful for being noticed. So after ten years of dwindling boycotts and peaceful demonstrations, how do you keep up the momentum—keep the movement alive—without going violent? Is this non-violent talk just an early stage in the movement, with the real fight for full Independence coming next?

Gandhi's answer was a more aggressive boycott: a less passive form of not buying and not paying taxes. He would force the issue publicly, in the streets and the fields of the entire country. But he needed a symbol of British oppression, something that everybody saw and everybody knew about, a symbol that could be violated without violence. The new target would be salt and the British tax on salt. The idea of non-cooperation with the British salt tax had come up in discussions several times before, but the idea was passed over because the salt tax was not a major source of revenue for the Empire. A boycott of salt would not hit the British where it hurt.

But the important target now was not the Empire; it was the Indian people themselves. Gandhi wanted to find a way to get the common people of India to show themselves that they were powerful politically. He wanted them to discover in themselves the great power of acting together. The Salt March, Gandhi stated, was "not designed to establish independence, but to arm the people with the power to do so."

There were large deposits of sea salt on the west coast of India, within his province of Gujarat, and within 240 miles of his ashram. Why not walk to the sea, gathering publicity and popular momentum all along the way? Why not deliberately break the law by gathering salt without paying the tax?

The salt tax would be the focal point of a new program of Satyagraha (truth-force). Refusing to pay the tax would not hurt the British financially, but wound them politically. As with the tax on tea in America, the real issue would not be a tax—the real issue would be the right to tax. Taxation is the right of any government; if you cannot tax, no matter how small the tax may be, you are not the government. In showing the mass of the Indian population how to defy the salt tax, Gandhi would show them how to bring themselves together to defeat British rule.

Insignificant as it was to the taxers, the salt tax was a burden on the poorest of the poor. "Next to air and water, salt is perhaps the greatest necessity of life. It is the only condiment of the poor." Gandhi wrote. "Cattle cannot live without salt...." Through the salt tax, the state could "...reach even the starving millions, the sick, the maimed and the utterly helpless. The tax constitutes therefore the most inhuman poll tax that ingenuity of man can devise ... 2,400 percent on the sale price! What this means to the poor can hardly be imagined by us.... [If] the people had freedom, they could pick up salt from the deposits made by the receding tides on the bountiful coast." In salt Gandhi had discovered the universal burden of the millions in India and vowed to overthrow it. "It was reserved for the British Government to reduce the curse to a perfect formula covering every man, woman, child, and beast."

But to actively involve the entire population, Gandhi could no longer rely on passive resistance. He would not only refuse to pay the tax, he would physically manufacture salt from the beaches of northwestern India. With several dozen hand-picked followers from his Sabarmati Ashram in Gujarat, he would march to the sea, pick up a wad of salt from the beach in violation of British law, and make salt: a small violation of a small tax with the symbolic power to move an empire.

Satyagraha began in March. Gandhi wrote to Viceroy Lord Irwin: "...if you cannot see your way to deal with these evils ... on the 11th day of this month I shall proceed with such coworkers of the Ashram as I can take, to disregard the provisions of the salt laws." Irwin "regretted Gandhi's decision, 'contemplating a course of action ... bound to involve violation of the law and danger to the public peace.'"

On March 12, 1930, with 78 other men, Gandhi began the 240-mile walk from the Sabarmati Ashram to Dandi's beach, to prepare salt in violation of the strict wording of imperial law. He told his followers they would only return to their homes "as dead men or as winners of swaraj" (self-rule). With hundreds of onlookers following along behind, the men left at 6:30 a.m., stopping to rest seven miles down the road. (Most of the original 78 made it all the way, though a dozen or so fell sick and returned to the ashram.) Women, children, and other interested onlookers were asked to turn back at the first stop. "Your way at present ... lies homeward," Gandhi told them. "Mine straight on to the sea-coast." Many women wanted an equal part in the march, but Gandhi (and others) thought that marching and camping with both men and women would be unacceptable to the wider society and a possible source of scandal.

But women continued picketing foreign dress shops and liquor stores. They remained active at the ashram and elsewhere in spinning, and in encouraging friends and family to wear khadi. "Perfect discipline and perfect cooperation among the different units are indispensable for success ... those who are not engaged in civil disobedience are expected to induce others to be engaged in some national service." Gandhi was talking here about women. "In this non-violent warfare, their contribution should be much greater than men's." Where women were rarely part of Satyagraha in the 20s, thousands became politically active for the first time in the 30s, and many were arrested along with men.

A Bombay chronical reporting on the scene further along the route reported, "Indescribable scenes of enthusiasm mark the progress of the march of the Swaraj [homerule] Army on this fourth day.... The rich and poor, millionaires and workers, 'caste' Hindus and so-called untouchables, one and all, vied with one another in honoring India's great liberator.... All castes, creeds, religions, and interests were merged into one irresistible wave of patriotism. All appeared a perfect Gandhi Raj.... The authority of the Government seemed to be almost nonexistent...."

The scene was cheerful and exuberant up close, but Gandhi never knew how many people across the country would actually refuse to pay the salt tax, refuse to buy salt, or illegally make it themselves. "If the salt loses its savour, wherewith shall it be salted?" He worried. "Students have no faith in self-sacrifice, and less in non-violence. Then naturally, they will not ... come out." He feared that students would remain in school, at home, or in their classrooms, ignoring his call to action. "Suspend your studies and join in the fight for freedom. When victory is won ... you will resume your studies in schools of our own government."

Every day and every night of the march Gandhi expected to be arrested. "Today we are defying the salt law. Tomorrow we shall have to consign other laws to the waste-paper basket." Each day the police failed to show, and he wondered why the viceroy was not taking the bait. What if the salt march was simply ignored by the authorities? This is another great worry of the Satyagraha organizer: what if you go to all the trouble of breaking a law and nobody notices? What if you beg to be arrested and the police just walk on by? So far the Viceroy was not playing his part in the drama. Perhaps he felt he could defeat Satyagraha by simply ignoring the non-violent offenders. Gandhi spun it as a weakness of the British rulers. "...The Government dare not arrest me. Why are you afraid of such a government? I have only 80 volunteers with me. Even then the government cannot arrest me. What then could it do if there were 80,000 volunteers?"

Information was distributed in advance to villages along the way about needs for food, water, and resting places. Gandhi also asked that written forms be filled out listing numbers of inhabitants and how many of them wore khadi or were operating spinning wheels. Some villages had none of either. Navagam, a town of one thousand, reported one khadi wearer and one active spinning wheel. The nation-wide excitement stirred up by the march was not translating into spinning wheels and homespun clothing.

Toward the end of the march, the numbers of followers grew every day. On April 6, Gandhi and 2000 other Satyagrahis walked onto the beach at Dandi, stood ankle-deep in the water for a few minutes, then walked back to the beach and picked up lumps of salt from the sand. The salt law was broken. As others on the march stooped to gather their own lumps of salt from the Dandi beach, people in other parts of the country began violating the salt laws in Bombay, Calcutta, Bengal, Tamil Nadu, and Kanpur. Gandhi had captured the imagination of the nation. But still no arrest. Others were being arrested across the country, but Gandhi was walking free. This was not the plan. To force the issue further, he would have to escalate. But how do you escalate non-violence?

A few hours down the road from Dandi beach was a British owned facility, the Dharasana Salt Works. After some thought, and perhaps frustration, Gandhi planned what he called a "raid" on the factory: salt marchers would storm the facility. What that meant, no one knew for sure, but this was no longer passive resistance. The "raiders" would be non-violent—strictly non-violent—but they would be "raiding." They would be pushing their way forward, non-violently, but all the while knowing the inevitability of violence against them. Participants would have no weapons and would not defend themselves against whatever blows they might receive. But they were going to advance on the facility. This is tricky. How do you advance into armed police power? The protestors were going to force their way in. Were they going to seize control of the factory? Shut it down? If successful, how would they maintain control without physically removing managers and workers? Or was this merely a show of force—of truth force?

Gandhi wrote a "Dear friend" letter to Viceroy Lord Irwin: "God willing, it is my intention … to set out for Dharasana and … demand possession of the Salt Works." The "raid," he said, could be prevented by the repeal of the salt tax. Greater repression on the part of police would be met by greater suffering on the part of his followers. Those killed and injured would be replaced by others. But as he finished the letter, and before he could send it, the police showed up and arrested him. Anticipating this, he appointed new leaders for the event and gave them strict instructions. Demonstrators were not so much as to raise their arms to protect themselves from attack.

With the news of Gandhi's arrest, hundreds of thousands poured into the streets of major cities, and thousands were beaten by police and arrested. Within days, every prison cell in India was filled with protestors. Gandhi re-stated his demands: repeal the salt tax and stop the importation of all foreign cloth. He asked the Viceroy to stop treating India as a slave nation: 300 million south Asians should no longer be held hostage by a distant island in northern Europe.

Two weeks after the arrest, a group of 2500 Satyagrahis approached the gate of the Dharasana Salt Works factory as thousands more stood by in witness. Four hundred native policemen with half a dozen British commanders surrounded the stockade, waiting for them. Twenty-five native riflemen stood ready at a distance. The entire group of protestors walked to within 100 yards of the stockade and halted. From within their midst, a single column continued the advance through the ditches in front of the stockade. Police officials ordered them to disperse. They continued to walk forward, slowly. Nobody knew what would happen.

A sudden command was given, and the police descended on the marchers. A United Press correspondent, Webb Miller, was there and reported what he saw: "Scores of native police advanced upon the advancing marchers, and rained blows on their heads with steel-shod lathis. Not one of the marchers even raised an arm to fend off the blows. They went down like ninepins.... In two or three minutes the ground was quilted with bodies. Great patches of blood widened on their white cloths. The survivors without breaking the ranks silently and doggedly marched on until struck down.... I could detect no signs of wavering or fear." Many of the fallen were unconscious, skulls were fractured and shoulders broken. Blood stained the ground. Thousands of witnesses groaned and sucked in their breath. After everyone in the first wave of demonstrators was knocked down others kept coming. Another wave followed, and another. Miller continued, "The police kicked and prodded the non-violent raiders who swarmed the depot.... The spectacle of them beating the unresisting volunteers was so painful [that] I was frequently forced to turn away from the crowd." Stretcher-bearers rushed in and carried away the wounded.

Another column formed and marched slowly toward the police without wavering. The police rushed forward and systematically knocked down the second column. There was no fight, no struggle, no outcry. Another wave of stretcher-bearers carried off eighteen wounded and then there were no more stretchers. Forty-two more people were left groaning on the ground. According to Miller, "Several times the leaders nearly lost control of the waiting crowd. They rushed up and down frantically pleading with and exhorting the intensely excited men to remember Gandhi's instructions. It seemed that the unarmed throng was on the verge of launching a mass attack on the police. The British official in charge, Superintendent Robinson of Surat, sensed the imminence of an outbreak and posted his twenty-five riflemen on a little knoll ready to fire." But the crowd remained in control of itself, "...detachments of police approached one seated group to disperse under the non-assemblage ordinance. The Gandhi followers ignored them and refused even to glance up at the lathis, brandished threateningly above their heads. On command, the beating recommenced coldly, without anger. Bodies toppled over in threes and fours, bleeding from great gashes on their scalps. Group after group walked forward, sat down, and submitted to being beaten into insensibility without raising an arm to fend off the blows. Finally, the police became enraged by the non-resistance (of) the demonstrators not fighting back. They commenced savagely kicking the seated men in the abdomen and testicles. The injured men writhed and squealed in agony which seemed to inflame the fury of the police, and the crowd again almost broke away from their leaders."

As he watched from a distance, Former Speaker of the Assembly, Vithalbhai Patel, said, "All hope of reconciling India with the British Empire is lost forever."

By 11 a.m., the heat reached 116 degrees in the shade and the demonstration was called off. There were 320 wounded. Two killed. The soldiers of Gandhi's peace force would die, but they would not kill.

No one had seen anything like this: thousands of men, in

formation, marching to war without weapons, without defense of any kind. This was the strangest battle in all history, and one of the most decisive. Tactically, it was a total failure. The "raiders" never made it to the gate, never got inside the building, and never came close to gaining control of the facility. But they won the awe and respect of the world. Their secret weapon was the media, in this case, newspapers. Eyewitness reports, like that of Webb Miller, at the engagement at the Dharasana Salt Works were telephoned to major cities all over the world. Suddenly anybody with a newspaper in their hand knew that something very exciting, and very new, was happening in India.

A police officer in South Africa, many years earlier summarized the effects of non-violent tactics on law enforcement: "How can we lay hands upon you? I often wish you took to violence like the English strikers, and then we would know at once how to dispose of you. But you will not injure even the enemy. You desire victory by self-suffering alone and never transgress your self-imposed limits of courtesy and chivalry. And that is what reduces us to sheer helplessness."

Gandhi remained in prison for the following nine months. At one time shortly after the Salt March began, there were around 100,000 Indians in jails throughout the country. Indians were paying the price for Satyagraha, the British were feeling the guilt, and beneath the surface, Gandhi was slowly winning the struggle. But India was not yet free.

In 1931, after Dandi and Dharasana, Gandhi traveled to England for "Round Table" talks on possibilities for home rule, dominion status, or complete independence. The British public knew him well and the press followed him everywhere he went. He met the King, the Archbishop of Canterbury, and many other personalities. The talks themselves were a complete failure, but Gandhi spent weeks afterward touring parts of England, winning over the hearts and minds of the British public. No one was sure, however, how he would be greeted in the manufacturing districts of Lancashire, where thousands of workers were unemployed due partly to the Indian boycott on British manufactured goods. There may have been some private resentment among workers, but Gandhi was greeted everywhere with open arms, seen more as a hero of the workingman, Indian or British, than as an economic opponent. Negotiations for independence may have been going nowhere, but Gandhi was becoming a folk hero in Britain and America, even France, and Satyagraha was winning the conscience of the elite and the common people of the western democracies.

Back home, with the independence movement stalled once again, Gandhi announced a new program of passive non-cooperation. Liquor stores and foreign clothing stores would be boycotted and picketed, illegal salt processing would be encouraged, and complete independence would be the goal. Civil disobedience would continue against all unjust laws. As Satyagraha once again took effect, Gandhi was arrested again, along with most of the leadership of the India National Congress, and the new Viceroy suspended civil rights for the entire population of India. Within four months, 60,000 protestors were in jail. Satyagraha and the drive for independence were essentially suspended during World War II.

Gandhi's position on warfare had evolved over the years. He never fought as a soldier, but did help organize an ambulance corps during World War I in support of the British war effort. He even helped recruit soldiers from the Indian population. But by the time World War II came about, after two waves of Satyagraha in India, Gandhi's views on nonviolence had deepened. His most extreme written statement on the subject of war appeared in a 1940 letter "to all Britons." He did not wish them defeated in the war with Germany, but suggested that Hitler and Mussolini should be allowed to "take what they want" of Great Britain. "If these gentlemen choose to occupy your homes, you will vacate them … you will allow yourself, man, woman, and child to be slaughtered." This was during the London Blitz. The idea did not take hold in Churchill's England.

A critic in London once wrote that Gandhi "is a problem. To Rulers and Governors, he is a thorn in their side. To logicians, he is a fool. To economists, he is a hopeless ignoramus. To materialists, he is a dreamer. To communists, he is a drag on the wheel. To constitutionalists, he represents rank revolution." We could add that to Hindus he was a disguised Muslim, and to Muslims, a no-good Hindu.

Gandhi is a problem for me, too. Do we need someone like Gandhi to inspire us to get off fossil fuel? Or do we need a more down-to-earth pragmatist—a scientist, say, or an economist? A politician, perhaps?

I like everything about Mahatma Gandhi: the clothing, the style, the otherworldliness, and the strength of character. There has never been anyone else like him. But I would keep him where he is: high on a pedestal in pre-war India, away from the current movement against fossil fuel. I like him as an ideal—a perfection—and at a distance. He doesn't belong in the modern world. He hated the modern world; maybe that's what we admire most about him. He floated above the ground he walked on and drew strength from an internal spirituality that ruled his every gesture. He was absolutely right about everything, especially the spinning wheel. If everyone would only spin for an hour or two every day, make everything by hand, and turn away from factory production, there would be work for everyone and we would all live simpler and better lives. We would deny ourselves the things that cause the trouble we are in. If we could all be like Gandhi, we would stop driving cars, stop heating houses, and learn to suffer it through. (In his own time, these were not the problem; Gandhi did not like cars, trains, and electricity, but he used them.) Following Gandhi's leadership, we would reject the modern world and go back to where we were before fossil fuel: problem solved! If going backward were a possibility, we should do it.

But it's not a possibility. The modern world is with us and will not go away. We can no more give up cars and computers, air conditioning, and electric lights than colonial India could give up power looms and spinning jennies. Life does not go backward. India never did give up its factories and never did accept the spinning wheel in daily life the way Gandhi had hoped. So no, we do not need Gandhi in our midst today. We don't need him telling us how to turn off light switches and recycle beer cans. We don't need him in the bedroom telling us what clothing to wear, and we don't need him at the dinner table telling us which bite to take. We need him at a distance, lifting us above everyday life to see the larger world beyond the immediate need. We need him showing us that we may have to suffer one day; that we can suffer successfully if we have to; that we can do without most of the stuff we think we must have; and that we can be happy and fulfilled without most of the stuff we do have. We need Gandhi to embody the ideal of discipline and commitment, refusing to consume the products that lead to dependence and slavery, be they foreign clothing or natural gas. But we need to learn the discipline ourselves, not accept it on authority, spiritual or otherwise. We need to see the reasons and feel the need, for ourselves, directly. We need the authority not of a charismatic individual, but of scientific consensus.

Gandhi's greater gift is to remind us that the ends do not justify the means. When the movement turned violent at Chauri Chaura, he stopped the movement. This was new. Everyone else wanted to say "sorry for the lives lost" and keep the movement going. But Gandhi knew that the means become the end. If you achieve everything you set out to do through violence, violence will be built into the society you achieve. Thanks to Mahatma Gandhi, progressive movements today almost universally begin with the assumption of non-violence. Violence is no longer an option; whatever we end up doing we will do it by non-violent means. Environmental movements, racial justice movements, indigenous rights movements, antiwar movements, etc., assume that aims will be best achieved, and goals more firmly established if tactics remain non-violent. In a democracy, the goal has to be winning over the general public—the people who care about justice, equality, and the environment, but who need to have the truth brought to the surface. If shown that a segregated bus means a segregated society, or that a salt tax is the exploitation of one people by another, people will gradually change how they live. The modern public turns away from violence and will not be forced to accept new changes in lifestyle that are brought about through brute force. This is a good thing. This is a sign of long-term progress in human affairs. It is not good that people remain docile and complacent, but it is good that people now reject any social or political change that requires violence. We have evolved to that extent. Non-violence is based on the repugnance we feel in hurting other people and being hurt by them, but it is also based on the effectiveness of non-violence in winning over the general public. Non-violent tactics bring truth to the surface. If done well, non-violent tactics help people see something they already know on a subconscious level but have never realized on a conscious level. A society can grow to a higher level of awareness through the power of Truth.

Human equality is an example of a truth that becomes evident through Satyagraha, through non-violent agitation. Satyagraha makes people in power look into themselves and see things they never knew were there. In India it made the British public see the injustice of imperialism. In Montgomery it made the white power structure see the injustice of a segregated society. The truth-force Gandhi spoke of brings protestors themselves to see a truth they may never have intended to show.

Climate change is another truth that can be shown with Satyagraha, perhaps only through Satyagraha. Climate change is not about personalities or politicians. It's not an opinion, not a hoax or a conspiracy. Climate change is a truth—a truth that not everyone can see. Through carefully considered and carefully executed acts of non-violent agitation, Satyagraha can bring the truth of climate change out into the open for everyone to see. It's there—all we have to do is point to it.

We also learn, in our travels with Gandhi, that purely passive forms of non-violence, like boycotts, can be boring and ineffective. Boredom is dangerous in that people who no longer feel the meaning behind the movement get tired of toeing the line, and eventually drop out of the boycott. Some sort of action is needed, now and again, to revive and sustain the passivity of constant non-buying. Something has to be done to remind people what they are not buying for. From time to time, a less passive form of non-violence must be incited, Gandhi found, to restore commitment. Dharasana is the consummate example of aggressive non-violence. People at the Salt Works not only refused to use violence, but they also offered themselves up to violence on the part of the oppressor and won the sympathy of the world. Many were seriously injured and some killed for what they believed, but the casualty figures pale next to those of other events in the twentieth century. Such exceptional levels of commitment can be expected only in extreme circumstances. Dharasana would never have happened without Mahatma Gandhi.

Many years after Gandhi's assassination in 1948, Bill Maudlin published a cartoon on April 4, 1968, after Martin Luther King's assassination. Gandhi was drawn sitting cross-legged, welcoming MLK to heaven, saying, "The odd thing about assassins, Dr. King, is that they think they've killed you."

Meanwhile: September 20, 2019

> *Several hundred students in the "Sunrise Movement" stayed away from school today and assembled in Jefferson Square Park in downtown Louisville for the global Climate Strike. There was one arrest at an intersection later in the afternoon.*

Meanwhile: September 25, 2019

> *It's been a big week for the U.N.*
>
> *In its latest special report, "The Ocean and Cryosphere in a Changing Climate," the Intergovernmental Panel on Climate Change (IPCC) announced that the ice caps are melting and the oceans warming and rising more rapidly than previously thought. The panel also announced a new phenomenon in the world's oceans: heatwaves. Concentrated bodies of warmer than normal water are forming with increasing frequency and intensity.*
>
> *Last Friday, 16-year-old Greta Thunberg of Sweden told the U.N. she didn't want them to listen to her; she wanted them to listen to the scientists. She's right about that. This is not about personalities, even hers, it's about what is happening in the world. She also stated that if world leaders really understood what was happening, as they claim, and did nothing about it, they would be evil, which she refuses to believe. She's right about that, too.*

> *Speaking at the U.N., one of those world leaders (as impeachment investigations began against him) claimed yesterday, "The future does not belong to globalists; it belongs to patriots." He's wrong. Greta has the more sophisticated worldview.*

Buses

I like to begin with Fred Gray. The great heroes of Montgomery were Ralph Abernathy, E.D. Nixon, Jo Ann Robinson, Martin Luther King, Jr., Robert Graetz, Rufus A. Lewis, and, of course, Rosa Parks. Many, many others brought this boycott to the level of a mass movement. But I like to begin with Gray, a 25-year-old attorney, fresh out of law school, with an office in the capital of Alabama.

Gray had lunch with Rosa Parks on Thursday, December 1, 1955, a few hours before she was arrested on a Montgomery city bus for disorderly conduct. We don't know what they talked about, or to what extent Gray and others might have known about Mrs. Parks' intentions, but later events prove that Gray had, or would develop, a much wider view than most of what would happen in Montgomery.

Rosa Parks' crime was not relinquishing her seat to a white passenger: a passive crime, a crime of not doing. Gray agreed to take her case. This was the third time a black woman had been arrested that year for violating segregated bus laws, but this time the black community rose up in arms—verbal, spiritual, compassionate arms. The community might have risen up violently but did not.

Things happened fast. The very night of Park's arrest Jo Ann Robinson, a professor at what is now Alabama State University, wrote up a pamphlet advertising a bus boycott. She and several others stayed up until 2 a.m. cranking out copies on an old mimeograph machine. The next day, barely 24 hours after the arrest, a meeting was called. Leaders (40–50) of the African American community decided to stage a one-day boycott of the Montgomery bus service the following Monday, December 5. The pamphlet was ready to go.

The issue of leadership came up in a flurry of meetings over the weekend. E.D. Nixon, a labor organizer and long-time leader in the Montgomery African American community, got the call from Rosa Parks and was at the center of events at this point. He called Gray, Robinson, and several others. Because the black community leadership was only loosely organized and somewhat divided by personalities, it was decided that a new locally controlled organization would be appropriate with a fresh face at the top. Martin Luther King, Jr., was the unanimous choice. At 26 years of age, King had become pastor of the Dexter Avenue Baptist Church only a year earlier. He rose to the occasion in a mighty way, speaking with bold spiritual and intellectual power at eye level with the common people.

Three things happened that Monday, December 5. A successful boycott began, Rosa Parks was convicted of her crime and fined $14, and the Montgomery Bus Boycott held its first mass meeting.

Publicity was so effective over the weekend that 90 percent of the African American community stayed off the buses on Monday. People showed up at their usual bus stops, but only to encourage others to comply with the boycott. Leaders were careful to keep boycotters from using any sort of coercion, though white police and city officials warned of black "goon squads" intimidating would-be bus riders. Car owners were asked to provide rides. Black cab owners reduced rates, and some whites provided rides for their domestic workers. Other boycotters simply walked to work or school. There was great comradery in the streets as people who had never met before suddenly felt a common cause and commitment. The Monday boycott worked better than anyone could have hoped. Organization, commitment, and practical alternatives to riding the bus were pivotal to its success. Things were so well organized on that first day, and commitment so strong, that when the decision came to extend the boycott, the entire community was ready for the long haul. The carpool was later organized with regular routes and fixed pick-up and delivery locations. At a central location downtown, riders coming in on one route could transfer to another outgoing route. Three hundred privately owned cars participated. Churches bought station wagons and hired full-time drivers.

Rosa Parks' case was heard in court on the morning of December 5. Eugene Lowe, the city prosecutor, said later: "It was a routine case that just came up. We didn't pay any attention to it. It wasn't a cause celebre one way or another in court." But Fred Gray saw it differently. He thought it would "...raise legal issues ultimately that would be decided by the United States Supreme Court." And it did.

The first mass meeting of the Montgomery Bus Boycott was held that Monday evening at the Holt Street Baptist Church. Ralph Abernathy reports that as he and King walked to the church they discussed whether or not to continue the boycott after the one-day success. It would depend on the turnout of the meeting. When 5000 people showed up, spilling out into the street, the decision was easy. Hands clapped, hymns were sung, prayers prayed, preachers preached, and people in the audience shared their experiences on the busses and in the streets. Spirits were so high that there was no question but to continue the boycott until grievances were resolved. Mass meetings, two each week, followed from then on and became the heart and soul of the movement. Meetings rotated among churches. Members of one congregation visited, sang, prayed, and shared stories with members of other congregations. Denominational differences were forgotten, and a common voice rose up from the black community.

King delivered the first speech. "...It is not enough for us to talk about love. Love is one of the pivotal points of the Christian faith. There is another side called justice. And justice is really love in calculation. Justice is love correcting that which revolts against love."

Love in calculation...

Early negotiations between boycott leaders and city officials focused on easing conditions on segregated buses. Each bus had a designated white section in the front and a black section in the back, with a middle section open to both races. But the law required blacks to leave their seats even in the middle of the bus if there were no more seats for whites in front. If there were no more seats anywhere, blacks had to give up their seats and stand, allowing whites to sit. The boycott called for eliminating the whites-only and blacks-only sections. Blacks would still be required to sit from the back forward, but they would not have to relinquish a seat once taken. Neither side budged in the negotiations. It is interesting to note at this point that desegregation was not the issue. As late as April 1956, King was saying, "We seek the right, under segregation, to seat ourselves from the rear forward on a first-come, first-served basis." The push was not yet toward an integrated bus, but toward a more equitable approach to segregated seating. Many white merchants supported a compromise, as they were losing business downtown. If either side had given in at this point, or if some halfway measure had been adopted, the larger matter of ending segregation on the local and national levels would not have come into question in Montgomery. The paradigm would not have shifted.

Mayor W.A. Gayle forced the larger question. "We are going to hold our stand," he said. "We are not going to be part of any program that will get Negroes to ride the buses again at the price of the destruction of our heritage and way of life." Heritage and way of life were the real issues. Meanwhile, violence and harassment began on the streets. The city could not make black people ride the buses, but they could make the alternatives more difficult. Police began selectively enforcing speed limits, overcrowding in cars, and parking and other minor traffic violations. (After nearly a year in operation, the carpool was declared illegal.) Martin Luther King was arrested for driving 35 mph in a 25 mph zone. In January of 1956, E.D. Nixon and Martin Luther King's homes were bombed. On February 10, the White Citizen's Council held a rally in Montgomery that drew 12,000 people. Later that month, 89 boycott leaders including Abernathy, King, Parks, Nixon, Lewis, Gray, and dozens of black ministers and community leaders were indicted for violating a state law against boycotts without "just cause." King was found guilty of conspiracy and fined $500 or 386 days of hard labor. He appealed immediately.

This is where Fred Gray's wider perspective comes into play. No doubt, recent Supreme Court decisions undermining segregation on the federal level were in the minds of other boycott leaders, but Gray led the way in this new direction. He reasoned that the Rosa Parks case was a matter of local criminal law: if they appealed for justice in her case, it would have to go through a lengthy process in the state court system before reaching the federal level. In any case, they might end up with no more than the Parks' conviction set aside (and the $14 returned?). Instead, Gray proposed filing a civil suit directly in the United States District Court in Montgomery. Other black leaders concurred. He and four other black lawyers then filed the federal suit on behalf of five other black women who had experienced racial discrimination on Montgomery buses. The suit was based on the Brown vs. Board of Education decision (1954), which ended legal segregation in public education. The Supreme Court had already decided that separate was inherently unequal: Gray's suit applied the same logic to public transportation (and thereby to all public accommodation). This is the wider legal significance of the boycott and why we remember it today. This is how a local issue became a national issue. Segregation was on its way out on the federal level, and the federal level was about to impose itself on Jim Crow heritage and way of life. Fred Gray saw the big picture.

But even bigger than Gray's big picture was the spiritual dimension of the Montgomery Bus Boycott. According to the Rev. Robert S. Graetz, a white pastor in Montgomery and only white member of the boycott leadership, the key to the boycott's success "was the role of love and nonviolence in Montgomery. Everything that grew out of what happened in Montgomery was influenced by that spirit. I am convinced that that is one reason Montgomery was able to withstand the other changes that came along." After King's home was bombed, a crowd of several hundred formed on the street outside, looking for revenge. Some were armed. King spoke to the assembled crowd, "We don't act like they do. They may treat us violently, but we are not going to do that." The crowd dispersed.

After all appeals were exhausted, the federal mandate ending bus segregation went into effect on December 20, 1956, and the bus boycott ended over a year after it had started. In calling off the boycott, King wrote, "Often our movement has been referred to as a boycott movement. The word boycott, however, does not adequately describe the true spirit of our movement. The word boycott is suggestive of merely an economic squeeze devoid of any positive value. We have never allowed ourselves to get bogged in the negative; we have always sought to accentuate the positive. Our aim has never been to put the bus company out of business, but rather to put justice in business."

King was very concerned about how blacks would interact with whites on newly integrated buses. He wrote up a list of suggestions, including:

In all things observe ordinary rules of courtesy and good behavior.
Remember that this is not a victory for Negroes alone, but for all Montgomery and the South. Do not boast! Do not brag!
Be quiet but friendly; proud, but not arrogant; joyous, but not boisterous.
Be loving enough to absorb evil and understanding enough to turn an enemy into a friend.
In sitting down by a person, white or colored, say "May I?" or "Pardon me" as you sit. This is a common courtesy.
If cursed, do not curse back. If pushed, do not push back.
If struck, do not strike back, but evidence love and goodwill at all times.
According to one's own ability and personality, do not be afraid to experiment with new and creative techniques for achieving reconciliation and social change.
GOD BLESS YOU ALL.

In January 1957, after the boycott had ended, four black churches and two black homes were bombed in Montgomery. There were no injuries. A shot fired at a moving bus struck a young African American woman in the leg. But intimidation and violence led to more support across the state, throughout the country, and across the world. White leaders were aware of this, and The White Citizen's Council even contributed to rewards for finding the perpetrators of violence. Some whites claimed that blacks themselves instigated violence to gain sympathy from a wider audience.

If you go to Montgomery today, you will find an historical marker on the street corner where Rosa Parks boarded the bus on that Thursday morning in 1955. You will find a Rosa Parks Library and Museum, complete with a mock-up of the bus, the street signs, and a video presentation of events as seen through the windows of the bus. The

Chamber of Commerce has claimed that Montgomery is the birthplace of the Civil Rights movement.

The world has changed.

What made this particular boycott so successful? Montgomery was a rare convergence of organizational, intellectual, tactical, and spiritual talent. Jo Ann Robinson and her group of educated black women saw the boycott coming. Within hours of the Parks arrest, Robinson wrote up a flyer and printed out thousands of copies that were distributed in black neighborhoods before even anyone had met to authorize a boycott. She might have wasted a lot of good mimeograph ink, but she and her group had the foresight and the gumption to take a chance, and there it was: a bulletin out the door, the morning after the Parks arrest. Rosa Parks, a mild-mannered seamstress and secretary of the local NAACP chapter, chose the right moment to stand (sit) her ground and became a great heroine of the twentieth century. Martin Luther King, Jr., saw the spiritual dimension of racial equality, tapped into the biblical struggle of the Hebrew people, and brought inspiration to the movement from Gandhi's non-violent struggle for independence a half-world away in India. And then there was Fred Gray, who was quick to apply the constitutional principle of equal rights for all Americans to a local quarrel over a bus seat.

This is how you change the world. You take a global issue: human equality, climate change, etc., and you bring it down to the local level. You look at what is going on in your town, your city bus, your local utility, your Public Service Commission, and you undertake actions on that level. Or, more likely, you build from the bottom up. You take a local issue: a pipeline, a shooting, a power plant, etc., and you find the global dimension. Not everyone will see it at first. But if it is there, if it is true, the global dimension will work its way to the surface. Think globally; act locally. Then, when the moment arises, act globally, too.

Montgomery had two other things going for it: a great narrative and a great symbol. This was an everyday story that everyone could relate to. In one way or another, we all work, we all get tired, we all ride the bus. Rosa was exhausted, just as you and I get exhausted from time to time. Nobody likes to stand up when there are empty seats on the bus. Nobody likes to be put down, insulted, and cursed.

With so much going on around them every day, some of the boycott's organizers may not have realized at first that a segregated bus would soon become a powerful symbol for a segregated society. The bus became a microcosm of the whole country, a symbol that all the world could see. Social and economic issues sometimes become so big and so complex that we lose sight of their simplicity. Equality is simple. You and I and the other guy are all the same thing. We rarely see the simplicity in a single image, but here, in Montgomery, the whole issue of segregation is presented in a single capsule: a city bus with white people in the front and black people in the back. This cannot exist in an equal society. We said we were supposed to be equal, right?

Finally, the Montgomery Bus Boycott had Truth going for it. If you are working for something that is true, that truth will become evident in time. Human equality is a Truth. People have racial differences, cultural differences, economic differences, and individual differences, but all people are fundamentally the same. All people are human. In an imperfectly developed society, cultural, economic, and individual differences are often confused with racial differences, but all races are equally intelligent, wise, and capable of learning. This is a timeless truth revealing itself everywhere in the modern world. It is a truth that came to the surface when a swarm of tired workers found the courage and strength to make their way on foot through the streets of Montgomery, Alabama, as a fleet of empty buses rolled past.

This is what Gandhi meant by Satyagraha—truth force. You don't have to make something true if it's already true. All you have to do is reveal it. You may not even know exactly what the truth is—you definitely will not know its full breadth. Rosa Parks, Fred Gray, and Martin Luther King, Jr., did not know that they would change the world the way they did. How could they have known? They did not know that the local newspaper would be interested in their story, or that the television station, and the reporters from Birmingham, Atlanta, Chicago, New York, London, Paris, and New Delhi would be interested.

Truth is much bigger than anything we can think and know. It is often something we only feel. Rosa Parks felt something true in her heart and in her tired feet that day in Montgomery.

You and I may never see the results of whatever actions we take to eliminate fossil fuel combustion in the Earth's atmosphere. We may never know what happens in the mid and late twenty-first century. But if we are on to something true—even if we do not fully understand it—the world will change.

100% REAL Update: September 27, 2019

The "Rally to Save Bernheim Forest" was held this afternoon in downtown Louisville. I spoke briefly, shouting out my favorite numbers to the crowd: 91!; 40!; and 6000! (From 2018's IPCC special report by 91 scientists from 40 countries who analyzed 6000 scientific studies of the Earth's climate, concluding that we have to be completely off fossil fuels in 30 years.) The fossil fuel pipeline LG&E wants to build through the forest preserve would still be operational 50 years from now!

The crowd marched from Jefferson Park over to the LG&E building. One demonstrator peacefully occupied an intersection and was arrested.

Meanwhile: October 2, 2019

The temperature yesterday hit a high of 97 here in Kentucky, six degrees hotter than the previous record for the day. New records are expected here again today and over the eastern U.S., another record is forecast for tomorrow. This could be understood as just another natural statistical variation, but climate is average weather, and so many statistical variations in the same general direction over the last few years amounts to an upward trend in average weather. In other words, climate change is here and it is now.

Apartheid

> "An exaggerated respect for the conqueror, his language, customs, morals, powers, rights … contempt for our countrymen and our language; a lack of faith in ourselves, our language and its durability, a low evaluation of our literature; a fear of being judged inadequate and ridiculed; a cowardly hypocrisy and imitativeness; and loss of the feeling of self- and national esteem."

These are not the words of a black South African describing white oppression; they are the words of a white South African (J.B.M. Hertzog) describing British oppression of his own white people, the Afrikaners. "Afrikaners" (not to be confused with black Africans) are white South Africans of Dutch descent, also known as Boers. It is they who created and sustained the Apartheid regime of 1948–94 in South Africa: a regime whose roots go back to 1647, one hundred and fifty years before the coming of the British. During the heyday of the Dutch Empire and before construction of the Suez Canal, control of the Cape region was of great strategic importance to European powers with interests in India, the Spice Islands, and the Far East. When the British took control of southern Africa in 1795, the Dutch became second-class white citizens in "their own" country, but were careful to maintain a strict sense of racial superiority over indigenous Africans, and later over immigrant Indians and mixed-race "coloured" peoples. South Africa became a meeting point of the world's major races: European, African, and Asian. But South Africa would not become a melting pot, as far as the Boers were concerned. The Afrikaner Dutch would stay a separate people despite extreme proximity to many kinds of people they were not.

Apartheid is a Dutch word meaning apart (pronounced "apart-hate"). It became a form of deliberate social engineering designed to keep whites in control of the country and, beyond that, to keep whites at a distance from other races to maintain racial and cultural purity. Most of the "coloured" people are mixed-race descendants of Boers and Africans, most speaking Afrikaans, a dialect of Dutch.

Other "coloured" are English-speaking mixed-race descendants of Dutch, English, Africans, Indians, or Indonesians. Many are descendants of slaves brought to southern Africa before the British Empire abolished slavery in 1834. Most "coloured" people live in Cape Colony in the southwest part of the country. Indians, both Hindu and Muslim, came between 1860 and 1911 to Natal Province in the northeastern part of the country, mostly as indentured workers. Many became laborers and shopkeepers. Black Africans occupied the country for thousands of years before the coming of the Dutch, English, or Indians. Ten separate tribes and many languages are recognized. At the beginning of the apartheid era (1948), Africans composed about 68 percent of the population, colored 9 percent, Indian 3 percent, and white (Afrikaner and British) about 20 percent. By the end of apartheid (1994) the Africans were up to 78 percent, "coloured" and Indians virtually unchanged, and whites down by half to about 10 percent. Throughout modern South African history, racial tensions have existed not only between blacks and whites, but between blacks and colored, blacks and Indians, and Indians and whites. Within the white portion of the population, the British defeated the Boers in a devastating war from 1899 to 1902, yet it was the Boers (Afrikaners) who prevailed over the British after 1948.

The British as well as the Dutch Afrikaners considered themselves racially superior to black Africans, but the British were less threatened economically and socially than Afrikaners. Where Afrikaners felt a need to fight to retain a privileged position, the British were more aloof in their contacts with other races and generally more liberal on racial issues. In the overall population, Afrikaners outnumber the British slightly and came to use that advantage to great effect. As the white population declined in relative numbers and more and more blacks were seen on the streets, both Afrikaners and the British felt a steady erosion of their position of white dominance in South African society. But it was the Afrikaners who led the way backward.

The story of apartheid is the story of urban migration after World War II. Segregation in a variety of forms existed in South Africa long before the 1940s, but most black Africans lived on reserves, or tribal homelands, while most Afrikaners lived on farms in rural areas. Blacks who worked in the cities were required to carry passes granting them temporary permission to live off the reserves. As stated by an official commission in 1922: "...natives—men, women, and children—should only be permitted within municipal areas in so far and for so long as their presence is demanded by the wants of the white population ... the masterless native in urban areas is a source of danger and a cause of degradation of both black and white."

At this time, "the wants of the white population" were mostly in the form of a desire for domestic workers. But World War II created a great demand for industrial urban workers, and the pass laws were suspended for the duration of the war. Thousands of blacks found work in the cities and made the move from their overcrowded homelands. After the war, segregation took on the extreme expression of apartheid as Afrikaners, many of them war veterans, returned home looking for jobs or moved to the city from the farm. Seeking industrial employment in the cities, Afrikaners soon encountered a large residual black population walking the streets, seeking the jobs Afrikaners themselves thought they had a right to. Laws were passed granting whites, or "civilized workers" the best jobs with several times the wages blacks received, and pass laws were reinstated. Black migrant workers were considered "temporary sojourners," allowed to be in town for as long as their labor was required. In theory, if you were black, you could not live in the city you worked in. If you had a pass, you could come to town to work, but only as long as you kept your job. If you lost your job, you lost your pass. Even if you kept your job, your wife and children were not allowed to live with you in town. They were forced to maintain husbandless, fatherless households back in the reserves. The theory was that you, and all other black people, would eventually return home to a tribal lifestyle natural to your racial competence, leaving the cities to the white people. In time, the theory went, all races would live entirely separately. Blacks would return to the forest, and whites would learn to live without black labor, industrial or domestic. At the end of every statement on racial policy, the public was reassured that "separate development" was best for black people, too.

But something very different was happening in the real world. A modern industrial economy was forming in the cities; populations, especially of black Africans, were swelling, and all sorts and conditions of people were moving from the country to the city. By law, whites received higher pay, but because they received higher pay, they were not as good a deal for employers. This became a sticking point between white employers and white politicians. Businesses wanted greater access to cheap black labor to lower production costs, while the government wanted to promote greater access to white labor. Pass laws were the politicians' attempt to reduce the number of Africans in town, thereby increasing opportunities for white Afrikaner laborers. White men, it was felt, should not be put in a position of competing with black Africans for jobs. The government, therefore, should do all it could to stem the tide of black labor pouring into the cities. But as Prime Minister Smuts quipped, "You might as well try to sweep the ocean back with a broom."

Apartheid was a more severe form of segregation than found in America. All unnecessary contact between races was banned by law. Some contact was unavoidable, but contact was never permitted on an equal basis. Competition in the labor market was made illegal and urbanization of blacks strictly regulated. Unions were allowed, but strikes and collective bargaining were banned for black Africans. In America, segregation was just the way things had to be; in South Africa, apartheid was an actively promoted campaign with a goal. The reason for apartheid was best summarized by an Afrikaner Prime Minister of the Transvaal: "The European had hitherto been able to maintain himself in South Africa because he was economically and culturally superior to the Native. If the Government went out of its way to civilize and uplift the Native in an unnatural manner, the White man would not be able to maintain his superiority." It hardly needs saying.

Apartheid was based on a static view of the black race: where whites could progress and evolve to higher levels of civilization, blacks were inherently tribal. They could be used, temporarily, on farms, or as migrant workers in urban factories, but they were biologically incapable of contributing to modern civilization. Within two or three generations apartheid would create an all-white society in all-white areas; blacks still encountered in these areas would become "foreigners" subject to deportation if their labor was not needed.

In 1946 the National Party, an ethnic Afrikaner party, appointed a committee to propose new government policies toward Colored, Indian, and African populations. The National Party was not then in power, but had held power briefly in the 1920s and remained in opposition during World War II. The committee recommended enforced segregation of all races, with strict penalties for violations of pass laws. Colored and Indian races were designated as alien and unassimilable. The colored had previously had the right to elect white representatives to the Natives Representative Council, but this right was to be abolished. Black Africans were to remain socially and economically segregated in native reserves, though provisions remained for allowing black labor on white-owned farms, mines, and factories. Black employment would be regulated by migrant labor laws. This committee's work was the origin of *apartheid*. The National Party was elected to office in 1948 and Dutch Afrikaners, 12 percent of the total population, gained control of the country and shaped it to their needs for the next half-century.

A major crutch provided to the National Party was the Cold War. All resistance to apartheid was labeled as "communist agitation," thereby assuring the government of British and American support for domestic policies. The Suppression of Communism Act of 1950 gave government ministers powers to "ban" individuals from belonging to certain organizations, from publishing books or pamphlets, or in some cases from leaving home. There would be no judicial interference with government authority and no reasons need be given for actions taken. Banned individuals had no right to appeal. Later legislation gave police the right to arrest suspects and hold them incommunicado, without trial, and in solitary confinement.

In 1952, a number of young blacks, inspired by Mahatma Gandhi's

Satyagraha movement in India, deliberately violated pass laws and went to jail voluntarily. They did not ask for bail and were willing to spend long terms in prison. But despite considerable sacrifice and bravery, violence broke out in the streets as police made the arrests, and the campaign was called off (as Gandhi would have done). The African National Congress (ANC) claimed the violence was not caused by their volunteers, but by police provocateurs. The campaign ultimately failed, but interest in the resistance movement increased as a result of it, and new public interest boosted ANC membership from about 7000 to over 100,000. The ANC Youth League (ANCYL) of which Nelson Mandela was a member, initiated a renewed program of resistance to apartheid including strikes, boycotts, and civil disobedience. In 1960 a protest over the pass laws broke out in Sharpeville. Police killed 69 black youths.

After Sharpeville, members of the ANC including Mandela himself felt that the era of non-violence was over. "I said it was wrong and immoral to subject our people to armed attacks by the state without offering them some kind of alternative.... Violence would begin whether we initiated it or not. Would it not be better to guide this violence ourselves...?"

The ANC formed a military branch known as *Umkhonto we Sizwe*, or MK. The original MK strategy was to target government buildings and installations, carefully avoiding loss of life. Railroads, police stations, and other symbols of oppression were bombed during off-hours when personnel would not be hurt. But the impact was minimal. The ANC leadership decided at that point to move toward more overt guerrilla warfare. Some recruits were sent abroad to Russia for training while others went to neighboring countries to the north where armed liberation movements were underway. The plan was to rely on the experience of returning recruits to build a guerrilla movement in South Africa. Trained guerrillas, it was hoped, would initiate an armed rebellion in South Africa, melting into the local population in rural areas between raids. African tribes were nominally in control of rural areas, and would naturally support the movement, much the way Vietnamese villagers supported the Viet Minh in guerrilla action against the French in Viet Nam. But tribal lands in South Africa were surrounded by white control, and setting up bases and establishing supply lines for the guerrillas proved impossible. Police infiltrated the group and arrested most of the MK leadership. The movement was crushed when the MK headquarters was raided and leaders were imprisoned or fled the country. By 1973 MK, though it had sent several hundred recruits to learn armed resistance in Zimbabwe, Mozambique, and Angola, had "not fired a single shot on South African Soil." MK troops abroad became bored and dispirited, anxious to return home and fight. Some blamed ANC leadership for the inaction, accusing them of becoming "professional politicians" instead of "professional revolutionaries."

Meanwhile in London, a group of African nationalists, Christian activists, and representatives from Afrikaner and South African Indian communities formed the AMM, or Anti-Apartheid Movement after the Sharpeville killings, organizing a boycott of South African goods. There were also movements abroad to isolate South Africa from international sports events. South Africa did not attend the Tokyo Olympics in 1964 and was expelled altogether from the Olympic movement in 1970.

The turning point of resistance to apartheid came in 1976 with the Soweto uprising outside of Johannesburg. Soweto began when the government imposed Afrikaans, the language of the oppressor, on all public schools as the language of instruction. High school students quickly formed the South African Students' Movement and organized a march of 15,000–20,000 people. Police used tear gas and then live bullets to break up the crowd, killing young students. The insurrection spread quickly. Before long, 176 were killed, according to government statistics, and 1139 injured. Protests spread from Soweto throughout the country: rioting, burning, stoning cars, and destroying government buildings. Boycotts and strikes were organized against white businesses and enforced by black youth. Seven hundred thousand workers stayed away from their jobs. By February 1977, after months of rioting, burnings, property destruction, and police shootings, 575 were dead.

Most of the unrest was spontaneous and unorganized, and the vast majority of rioters were students and young adults. The African National Congress was unable to control the rioting, but people nonetheless looked up to the ANC for leadership. Membership doubled several times over. After the Soweto uprising died down, the MK guerrilla wing of the ANC saw a revival in recruitment as young people caught up in the riots wanted to learn how to fight back against white control.

By the 1980s, the African population was growing much faster than white populations, and urban migration was ongoing by both blacks and whites. The Afrikaner population was becoming more urban, more highly educated, more sophisticated, more traveled, and more sensitive to world opinion. Skepticism of political authority was growing, particularly among young Afrikaners influenced by rock music and the youth movement in Britain and America. The border war with Namibia and military conscription were alienating many young Afrikaners and Afrikaners in general were becoming less hostile to the English. By the 70s and 80s, resentment over the British victory in the Boer War was finally dwindling, and intermarriage with the English became common. Roughly a quarter of English speakers had joined Afrikaners in supporting the National Party in country-wide elections, but overall, both English and Afrikaner were becoming more influenced by world opinion. Afrikaner incomes were still below those of the British, but were increasing significantly, and the Afrikaner sense of inferiority to the British had largely dissipated.

Censorship in literature and the arts was slowly relaxed, and public media allowed anti-apartheid voices to be heard. The Dutch Reformed Church had always upheld apartheid, but by the 1980s many theologians were seriously questioning the often-touted Christian foundations of apartheid. Recognition of the moral costs of racism led to open expressions within the church of an underlying social guilt

Business interests felt held back by apartheid. White capital investment was not allowed in the homelands, employers were forced to hire more expensive Afrikaner labor, and marketers felt restricted when asked to concentrate only on the white population. Arbitrary authority and the government expense of apartheid bureaucracy led to growing entrepreneurial resistance to the regime. Businesses wanting to expand across color lines and across national boundaries felt hemmed in by apartheid. As time went on, business, especially big business, found itself at the forefront of white resistance to apartheid. Overseas divestment programs and economic sanctions were beginning to take their toll on the South African economy.

The economy of South Africa experienced negative growth in 1982 and 83. In 1985, it sank by 1.2 percent. In 1986, growth was flat, inflation was in double digits, and high interest rates dampened investment.

Violence returned in 1984, again mostly aimed at the pass laws. A dispirited government repealed the pass laws in 1986, thereby undermining the central pillar of apartheid rule. The government's attempt to stem urban migration of blacks had to be abandoned. Even laws prohibiting mixed marriage were repealed. Schools remained segregated for the most part, but gradual desegregation seeped into hotels, restaurants, cinemas, and transport facilities, often forced on unwilling authorities through strikes and boycotts. Right-wing whites pushed back, often fomenting racial violence in the streets. Urban guerrilla attacks by MK operatives increased throughout the late 1980s. But the National Party regime remained steadfast, as apartheid crumbled around it on all sides.

P.W. Botha, Prime Minister at the time, refused to grant the vote to black Africans. A state of emergency was declared in 1985 and became permanent until 1990. Arrests without warrants continued by the hundreds, meetings were banned and broken up, and brutal police interrogations often ended in torture. Police powers were extended and press freedoms limited. According to author Jacques Pauw, after the state of emergency was declared, "The security forces were given extraordinary powers to counter the tide of black resistance. As a result, a new culture took hold in the security forces—one of no accountability and no rules. This soon bred an evil offspring— death squads. These units were never officially formed or sanctioned by the political leaders, but the fruits of the 'total strategy' were soon evident. Anti-apartheid activists disappeared and were mysteriously killed."

The violence continued nevertheless. Population expansion in the homelands forced more people off the land and into urban areas. Several hundred thousand were arrested every year. Some segregation laws were repealed; bans on multiracial political parties and interracial marriage were removed. Business centers opened up to blacks in some cities. Interracial sports events were allowed. Black wages increased and funding for black education was increased. President P.W. Botha admitted at one point that South Africa had outgrown apartheid. But despite these developments, society was still structured along racial lines, schools were still segregated, and millions of blacks were still unemployed.

In 1983 a thousand delegates of all races came together to found the United Democratic Front (UDF) to combat apartheid. Commuter bus boycotts, school boycotts, and rent strikes were organized, but also sabotage and violent demonstrations. An organized walkout of miners erupted into violence and led to the deaths of 175 people. By 1986, 240,000 workers were on strike and another 879 had died at worksites and in the streets.

Television in Britain and the U.S. showed the violence in the townships with video footage of soldiers and police beating and shooting unarmed blacks. As the regime felt growing pressure from overseas it reacted by banning further television and radio coverage of the riots. Although both British Prime Minister Thatcher and President Reagan opposed sanctions, divestment, and other anti-apartheid measures, antiapartheid sentiment increased in both countries. Public pressure mounted in Britain and America for business and government opposition to the National Party regime in South Africa. "South Africa," Reagan naively claimed, "has eliminated the segregation we once had in our own country." But a divestment movement was already spreading across America, and dozens of American companies were pulling out of South Africa. Economic growth there came to a standstill.

In 1986, the Comprehensive Anti-Apartheid Act passed in the

United States over President Reagan's veto. The Act made all new investment in South Africa illegal, restricted imports from South Africa, eliminated direct flights to and from South Africa and the U.S., called for political change, and demanded the release of Nelson Mandela from prison. Claiming South Africa was "unattractive for doing business," 120 companies divested, including General Motors, Xerox, General Electric, Exxon, and Coca Cola. The United Nations established an arms embargo and OPEC maintained an oil embargo. The South African economy was isolated and damaged, but held up through the crisis as local capital and management often bought up divested stock shares at fire-sale prices. The withdrawal of international banks proved most effective in punishing the apartheid regime. But the overall effect of divestment was more damaging psychologically and politically than economically. Divestment gave the regime an unwelcome and overpowering sense of global isolation and let anti-apartheid activists know that the world was on their side.

In 1989 Botha resigned as Prime Minister and National Party leader, turning over the government to Frederik Willem de Klerk. De Klerk, originally a hardliner, realized that apartheid was no longer tenable. Instead of continuing the repression, he sought as smooth a transition as possible to majority rule, protecting white interests to the extent possible. The ban on opposition organizations was lifted, and preconditions for negotiations with the African National Congress were established. Political prisoners were released from jail. After 27 years in prison, Nelson Mandela was set free.

Although De Klerk and Mandela did not like each other and did not get along well in private, it was their relationship that brought about the resolution that ended the violence. Both leaders were committed to a transition of power. Preliminary negotiations began in 1992 and continued for the next two years as both sides jockeyed for position and interracial violence continued to sweep through the country. Both de Klerk and Mandela had sizable opposition within their own parties, some Afrikaners seeing de Klerk as a traitor to his race, and many blacks clamoring for armed rebellion against continuing white rule. Black on black violence erupted when Zulus wanted independence from neighboring African tribes. Mandela traveled through Europe and the U.S. during the lead-up to negotiations, gaining enormous new support for the liberation of South Africa. Meanwhile, de Klerk's position continued to erode at home. But the deadlock continued; the resistance was unable to topple the state, and the state was unable to eliminate the resistance. Neither side was going to win through violence, and neither side was benefiting as violence continued.

In 1985 Mandela observed, "I had concluded that the time had come when the struggle could best be pushed forward through negotiations. If we did not start a dialogue soon, both sides would soon be plunged into a dark night of oppression, violence and war.... We had been engaged in the armed struggle for more than two decades. Many people on both sides had already died. The enemy was strong and resolute. Yet even with all their bombers and tanks, they must have sensed that they were on the wrong side of history. We had right on our side, but not yet might. It was clear to me that a military victory was a distant if not impossible dream. It simply did not make sense for both sides to lose the thousands if not millions of lives in a conflict that was unnecessary. They must have known this as well. It was time to talk."

When Mandela was let out of his cell after a long prison term, a prison officer offered him a kind remark. Mandela noted, "It was a useful reminder that all men, even the seemingly cold-blooded, have a core of decency and that if their hearts are touched, they are capable of changing."

Patrick Lekota, an ANC leader and one of Mandela's fellow prisoners, was especially interested in avoiding counter racism as negotiations continued. "In a political struggle," he said, "the means must always be the same as the ends. How else can one expect a racialistic movement to imbue our society with a nonracial character on the dawn of our freedom day? A political movement cannot bequeath to society a characteristic it does not itself possess."

That bears repeating: "A political movement cannot bequeath to society a characteristic it does not itself possess." The end does not justify the means.

114

An interim constitution was at last agreed upon and elections set for April 27, 1994. A final constitution and Bill of Rights would be prepared for 1996. De Klerk wrote in his journal, "We have shown that it is possible for people with widely differing views and beliefs to reach basic and sound agreements through compromise, through reasoned debate, and through negotiation."

About one million black youth had participated in mass protests, and the ANC was on the path to state power.

The economic pressure brought to bear by divestment and economic sanctions was marginal until 1985 when Chase Manhattan Bank began calling in loans and refusing to issue new ones. Under heightened antiapartheid pressure from shareholders and campus activists, the bank claimed that its motives were not political, and that it was withdrawing from South Africa, not due to apartheid but increased risks caused by the social instability. Because the South African economy was highly dependent on foreign investment the impact of the bank's withdrawal rippled through the business and labor communities. Accompanying the pullout of Chase and other foreign banks, domestic South African capital was also fleeing the country to overseas markets. General Motors withdrew in 1986, selling its operations to a local company.

Opinion polls among white South Africans showed that a near three-quarters majority felt that economic sanctions from foreign countries were hurting their country. Middle-of-the-road white citizens were feeling the pressure from the outside world. But many right-wing white politicians remained defiant, and actually benefited from domestic reaction to the sanctions and divestment. Archbishop Desmond Tutu argued that sanctions were the only possible means of avoiding a violent outcome to the crisis. The ANC and labor unions remained ambivalent about sanctions and divestment, as they often impacted employment.

But what was the overall effect of international sanctions? There is no doubt that they had some economic impact, but was it decisive? The economy was already at a standstill when divestment was fully underway, and it is quite clear that the real pressure on the regime was domestic: Sharpeville, Soweto, MK, and one million young people openly refusing to live their lives under a racist ideology. This was the muscle that brought about the end of apartheid. But would the apartheid regime have persisted if the divestment campaign had not begun? Were economic sanctions effective economically, or was their impact merely psychological?

International opposition began as soon as apartheid was implemented in 1948. By 1951, NAACP president Walter White was working to oppose World Bank loans to South Africa. There were protests against shipments of South African goods and demonstrations against bank loans to South Africa. In 1962, the U.N. issued Resolution 1761, which called for economic sanctions on South Africa, though it never received much support from western powers. In 1970, African American workers at Polaroid protested the company's involvement with the apartheid pass system. During the 1970s, activists began a *Boycott Gulf* campaign to protest the Gulf Oil Company's support of Portuguese colonial rule in Africa. Union workers around the country began refusing to unload ships carrying Rhodesian chrome. But, aside from diamonds and gold, there were few consumer products from South Africa to boycott. The economic weapon of choice against apartheid would not be a consumer boycott, but *divestment*, or the removal of capital from South African industry, by unloading stocks and calling in bank loans.

The 1976 Soweto uprising was a catalyst for new energy and sustained protest in the U.S. and Britain. Most campuses saw heightened activity after Soweto. Local coalitions, candlelight vigils, picket lines, and organizational caucuses against apartheid multiplied across North America. College students took over buildings and walked out of class in solidarity with their South African counterparts. When the apartheid regime's brutality reached a new level in 1984, the Free South Africa Movement engaged Americans from all walks of life in daily demonstrations and civil disobedience for more than a year. Shantytowns sprung up on college campuses that had not yet disinvested, and an international campaign against Royal Dutch Shell was launched in 1986.

Divestment began to affect South Africa as corporations let apartheid leaders know that it had become too expensive to continue operating there. Some observers would argue that corporations often blunted their ostensible activism through indirect investments in South Africa or by shifting ownership to local companies. But American banks provided something that could not be provided locally: capital. They caused some real pain when they refused to renew loans. The value of the Rand dropped immediately.

As pressure developed in churches and on college campuses to divest stock portfolios, some confusion arose among corporations as to what constituted support for apartheid. Just pulling out without considering consequences might cause harm in the wrong places. To provide some clarity, a set of principles was drawn up by the Rev. Leon H. Sullivan, an African American on the board of directors of the General Motors Corporation. The code he established called for corporations to observe the following principles:

- Principle 1—Nonsegregation of the races in all eating, comfort, and working facilities.
- Principle 2—Equal and fair employment practices for all employees.
- Principle 3—Equal pay for all employees doing equal or comparable work for the same time.
- Principle 4—Initiation and development of training programs that will prepare, in substantial numbers, blacks and other nonwhites for supervisory, administrative, clerical, and technical jobs.
- Principle 5—Increasing the number of blacks and other nonwhites in management and supervisory positions.
- Principle 6—Improving the quality of employees' lives outside of work in such areas as housing, transportation, schooling, recreation, and health facilities.

These principles prompted over one hundred American companies to divest from South Africa. The Sullivan Principles were effective in providing a basis from which corporations could evaluate investment decisions. They also provided activists on college campuses a set of guidelines they could use when pressuring administrators to divest. When financial advisors and managers of endowment and retirement funds communicated with corporations about the pressures they were feeling from their clients, they were able to point to the concrete written terms of the Sullivan Principles in determining which investments perpetuated apartheid and which did not. The great weakness of the Sullivan Principles was that they had no means of enforcement within South Africa itself.

The divestment movement was concentrated on university campuses, and in churches, unions, state and local governments, individual investors, and finally in the U.S. federal government. The first college to fully divest its holdings in South Africa was Hampshire College in 1977. Some said the gesture was merely symbolic, as the college's total divestment amounted to $ 39,000. But symbols are extremely important. The Hampshire move was quickly followed by nearby Amherst College and the University of Massachusetts. Later in the same year at Stanford University, 294 demonstrators were arrested at a campus sit-in demanding divestment of 93,950 shares of Ford Motor Company owned by the university. The university stood firm against the students and refused to agree to divestment until the movement was fully underway in the 1980s, and even then only agreed to partial divestment. The University of Wisconsin divested its $14,000,000 South African portfolio in 1978.

After organized student pressure on its East Lansing campus in 1979, Michigan State University sold $8.5 million worth of stock in thirteen companies. The university did not suffer financially by redirecting its portfolio but did see a drop in corporate donations from Dow Chemical, Ford, and General Motors, all of which did business in South Africa. Harvard University proved more intransigent. After Soweto, Harvard students built a shantytown in front of University Hall and forced the cancelation of a 350th-anniversary celebration in 1978. Selective divestment of its $400,000,000 South Africa related stock ensued. Nineteen students and one faculty member began a hunger strike in 1983. But Harvard never fully divested, claiming it would be costly and ineffective, and possibly damaging to African workers. In an open letter, President Derek Bok stated that the purpose of a university was to protect its financial stability and transmit knowledge, not to reform society. Many others on college campuses agreed. There was a general feeling then (and now) that making money in the stock market should have nothing to do with the conditions under which that money is generated. Business is about business: a business exists to make profits for its owners, not to make moral judgments. Yale and Columbia Universities, meanwhile, elected to divest completely.

The National Council of Churches governing board declared support for ending all economic collaboration between the United States government and South Africa and called for the withdrawal of funds from financial institutions with investments in South Africa. It also called for a ban on loans to the South African government. The AFL-CIO Executive Council called for all American corporations and affiliates to divest from South Africa and to sever ties with locally owned enterprises within the country. The United Auto Workers announced it would withdraw funds from institutions making loans to South Africa. More than 2,000 state, local, regional, and national organizations in the U.S with up to $100,000,000 of investment power announced that they would take some sort of financial action against apartheid. Nearly every major U.S. bank stopped lending to the South African government. Organizations within 35 of the 50 states in the U.S developed anti-apartheid programs, and the U.S. Congress passed the *Comprehensive Anti-Apartheid Act* in 1986, banning new bank loans and investments, plane flights, and many imports from South Africa.

In an editorial in 1980, the *Rand Daily Mail* recognized the danger that the U.S. divestment movement posed for South Africa, even admitting that divestment condemned apartheid, but questioned whether those instigating it knew the consequences of their actions. It warned that divestment foments widespread social unrest, which would work against a peaceful resolution of the conflict. The only way to save the country, the paper stated, was through rapid economic development and "meaningful change," (whatever that meant).

The great weakness of divestment from apartheid was that it could not restructure South African society directly. College students, clergy, and individual investors applied pressure on administrators and financial managers to apply pressure on corporations doing business in South Africa. The corporations would in turn apply pressure on South Africa society to reduce or eliminate racial discrimination in employment and working conditions. Much of the intended effect was lost in translation. Lack of capital often led to unemployment among the very people disinvestment was designed to help. The overall effect was to damage the economy of the apartheid regime, but divestment could accomplish its goals only as a blunt instrument punishing all members of society. Business opportunities and jobs were lost all around.

This unfortunate consequence of divestment in South Africa is not a likely outcome of the current divestment movement against fossil fuel companies, however, because economic effects in the current movement can be more specifically targeted. The stocks of companies involved in oil, gas, and coal industries can be sold directly within the economies that consume their products. Wage-earners, managers, and owners within particular industries will be affected adversely, but the economies within which they operate will be in a position to transition capital to renewable sources of energy. New investments will stimulate new, more appropriate forms of enterprise and employment. Divestment, along with a consumer boycott on fossil fuel products and continuing pressure on the government, will prove a major weapon in the fight against climate change.

Was the divestment movement effective in helping to abolish apartheid? Definitely! But it was not the death knell to apartheid that many in the West thought it was. Apartheid was abolished by South Africans themselves: black, white, "coloured," and Indian. Although the economic effects of divestment were clearly felt by South African businesses, by government, and by society as a whole, the most important and decisive effect was not economic, but psychological.

Divestment showed that apartheid simply did not, and would not, fit into the modern world. To persist in maintaining an avowedly racist regime, South Africans would not only have to continually struggle against violent racial unrest in the townships; they would have to exist isolated from the rest of the world. Modern South Africans, especially young people, were tired of being shunned by foreign visitors, business associates, media commentators, and sports associations. They wanted to be part of the modern world and not exist as a pariah nation when other countries were moving forward. Giving up the racial separation they were used to was a price worth paying to gain full membership in the larger world. As in the cases of King's Montgomery and Gandhi's India, being human proved a more powerful identity than being a type of human.

It strikes me that in all of these examples, with the exception of Montgomery, the boycott was secondary. Non-cooperation, non-importation, non-purchasing, and non-investment remained in the background of the decisive moment, the high drama, and the final victory: The Boston Tea Party, the Salt March, the Soweto uprising get the credit for changing the world. The long-term hard work of keeping a boycott organization active and focused is usually overshadowed by high-profile events in the street. Thus it seems probable that the carbon boycott alone will not accomplish all that is needed. If we are to succeed in ending the fossil fuel age, we must combine the boycott with other forms of pressure on governments and industry.

Looking more closely at each movement, the boycott aspect becomes inseparable from the events in the street that get all the attention. A boycott is always an expression of a strong, long-term community effort. A tight-knit group of people who share a compelling common purpose and who maintain constant contact with one another is necessary to produce a leadership that can define the objects and objectives of a boycott, maintain interest in the movement, and provide on-going support for the sacrifices it requires. It is this community-based consciousness that is also behind the dramatic events that bring about change.

So in addition to rerouting money from fossil fuels to alternative energy sources, the boycott serves to keep the community unified in intervals between public events. Although we tend to think that the community creates the boycott, it may be that the boycott creates the community. The constant drumbeat of the boycott society, day after day, year after year, and decade after decade keeps the movement going and keeps activists prepared to take decisive action when the time comes. There would be no Tea Party without a tea boycott.

It occurs to me also that a boycott need not be decisive economically. It must do damage economically—it must be effective—but it need not bring about the ultimate ruin of the opposition. It only needs to isolate the opponent from general acceptance in the larger society. If a fairly small sector of society can concretely demonstrate that it *will not* accept or buy into apartheid, segregation, British oppression, or the continued use of fossil fuels, that small group will inspire a larger sector of society to realize the truth it is expressing. And if the *Silent Majority*—that vast midsection of any society—is made to see a simple truth in recognizable form, it will change what it thinks, how it acts, and who it is. Once the Silent Majority has seen the truth and changed its mind, the opposition becomes isolated. Colonial Englishmen become Americans; Indian subjects become Indian citizens; black Americans sit in restaurants and buses and classrooms, and apartheid finds itself neutralized in a sea of human equality.

The boycott creates the community that inspires the society that changes the world.

If enough of us stop buying carbon, the rest of us will notice.

Meanwhile: October 26, 2019

Santa Ana Winds in Southern California and Diablos in the north are stoking over a dozen horrific wildfires in California. Hundreds of thousands of residents are forced to evacuate. Fires are also burning in eastern Australia.

Meanwhile: November 6, 2019

An article in the Journal Bioscience reports that over 11,000 scientists from around the world have signed a proclamation that the Earth is facing a "climate emergency." The current trajectory of climate change will lead to "untold suffering" for humanity and other forms of life. This is the first statement by a large group of scientists affirming that climate change is caused predominantly by human activities.

Meanwhile: November 11, 2019

Bush fires rage through Queensland and New South Wales in eastern Australia. Fires are common here, but the current blaze is larger, more intense, and earlier in the season than usual.

6

People First

The age of America First is over.

I just have to say this.

It has to do with the climate, sort of.

Don't get me wrong. Do not get me wrong! I love this place. This is my favorite country. I've traveled around a bit. I've seen other places. They are all beautiful in their own ways. But this is my country. I was born here and have lived here all my life. Maybe it's just that I was raised here, but I like this country the best, by far. I would not live anywhere else. I tear up at the amber waves of grain and the purple mountains in the distance. In my mind, I see images of the fruited plains in deep shades of red, white, and blue. That is what beautiful is! Brotherhood from sea to shining sea! I was with Francis Scott Key, peering over the ramparts at the rockets' red glare, wondering ... wondering ... if at sunrise I would still see the broad stripes and bright stars waving over the land of the free and the home of the brave. The brave! The people who would give their lives for this new sort of country! America was fragile then; would America make it through the night? It might have fallen, but here we are!

But far more than the red glare of rockets and the purple mountains, I love the institutions we have created and the ideals we have enshrined here in America: representative democracy, personal freedom, opportunity, and freedom of speech, press, religion, and expression. I cherish the federal constitution. What a work of human genius! Thirteen separate, quarrelsome, sovereign states voluntarily donating their powers to a single, central, national, American government—a wholeness so much more than the sum of its parts! I love the way we developed the balance of powers and saw far enough into the future to build safeguards against the tyranny of one-man rule. Then we came up with specific limits beyond which the government could not go. I love the assertion in the Declaration of Independence that the whole purpose of government is to protect these rights. I love the proposition, conceived in liberty, that all men are created equal. What a piece of work! And I appreciate above all Lincoln's remark that the Civil War in America was "testing whether that nation, *or any nation* [emphasis mine], so dedicated and so conceived can long endure" and his resolution "that government of the people, by the people, for the people, shall not perish from the earth." Not just from America—from the Earth.

America is unique. Not exceptional—*unique*. There is no other place on earth like it. Our ideas, our institutions, our way of merging into a united national community is one of the brightest moments in human history. I am proud to be American.

America became the first truly non-aristocratic society in human history. Everywhere else, people were born into the positions they held. We have always had a commercial aristocracy here, but it is not hereditary in any legal sense. I worry that it is becoming hereditary—that it may devolve into a form of commercial feudalism as capital and privilege become concentrated in the hands of the few—but theoretically, you can still grow up to be anything you are capable of being.

The ideas, the institutions, and constitutional rules that became modern America are unique, but they are not ours to keep. They happened here before elsewhere, but they do not belong to us alone. They are American in origin, but not in application. They are *human* values emerging all over the world. Democracy is a global value. Personal freedom is a universal value. Constitutional government has become the norm of national government the world over. A free democratic society is never a given, but all people everywhere are capable of achieving it. When they do achieve it, they will do it their own way. They have our example, but they will create their own society in their own way, not ours. We have a bad habit of criticizing other countries for being unAmerican. We are unique, but not exceptional.

We in America are closest to people who are closest to us. Like everybody everywhere, we are not sure we can trust those who look, dress, and speak differently. In this respect, we are not unique. Fear of foreigners, immigrants, and those of other races, religions, and ideologies is a trait Americans share with all other people. Fear of others is a global reality. People everywhere are wary of differences.

But appreciation of diversity is an emerging value; we are learning to value differences. We have to live with others so we might as well value them, as a practical matter. Differences are interesting. They make your world bigger … make you a bigger person—give you more reach. And when you find a glow of humanity under the scarf, or the turban, or the skin, your heart awakens. When you struggle to learn another language or listen to someone struggling to learn yours, the brotherhood—the sisterhood—will stretch from sea to sea and beyond. Humanity runs deeper than nationality, thankfully. Diversity can enrich life, but diversity is more than that; diversity is a survival mechanism. There is no other way to continue living on the Earth. *Humanity runs deeper than the differences.*

And the climate?

One line of questioning goes: Why should we protect *our* climate while people in Russia and China and Timbuktu refuse to protect *theirs*? We're only four percent of the Earth's population—why should we be the ones to regulate our behavior while everybody else keeps dumping more carbon dioxide and methane into the atmosphere?

Those are bad questions. There is no good answer to a bad question. A better question: Who is the *"we"* that needs to protect the climate?

America? That's a bad answer to a good question. There's no point in America, *or any nation* so dedicated and so conceived, regulating its own atmosphere. That's not going to work. National governments divided against each other are not capable of managing climate change effectively. An America First approach—even with a really good climate policy—can do no more than correct four percent of the problem. Sure, "if everybody else would only..." but everybody else won't. Some will, but not everybody else. If everybody would only quit cheating on their taxes and pickpocketing on the streets, we wouldn't need auditors and police. We need global vision here, global policy, and global enforcement. The world as a whole has to manage the atmosphere as a whole. Simple. That is the way it is. Yes, we still need national government. Global unity does not erase national boundaries, and we can still be proud of our separate traditions, but nationality comes second, not first. America is no longer first! America is cool, but no longer first.

Climate change is the first truly global crisis to face humanity. We have to unite, as people, to deal with this problem, in order to survive. Yes, survive. We have to evolve in ways that we may not like and may not have intended. If we like and intend them, it will be easier. That is reality. That is the way it is.

Climate change is not the only global crisis, just the first one. There is no national solution to nuclear weapons either—except more nuclear weapons. There is no national solution to overpopulation, contagious disease, world trade, industrial pollution, deforestation, major disaster relief, or oceanic pollution, to name a few. The Age of America First, China First, India First, or Nigeria First is over. Nationalism is no longer relevant. All of our existential challenges now are global, not national.

America is cool. It's still the Age of America in many ways, but no longer the Age of America First. This is the Age of People First. All people everywhere. First.

Get used to it.

Meanwhile: November 12, 2019

> *Record low temperatures here today and in the forecast for tonight. This, after record high temperatures last month.*

7

Divestment as a Power Tool

Divestment (disinvestment, divestiture) is integral to the carbon boycott and integral to the formation of community-based boycott organizations. If we are refusing to buy the products of the fossil fuel industry, there is no question that we should be refusing to capitalize on the fossil fuel industry. Divestment is effective and relatively easy. Just sell whatever shares you own.

But what constitutes a share in the fossil fuel industry? A share in Peabody Coal? Obviously, but what about General Motors? What about airlines, agribusiness, and fast food chains? Where do you draw the line? And more importantly, what do you buy instead? It takes a lot of time and research to invest conscientiously. I just checked my own modest portfolio and found that what I assumed was a totally carbon-free mutual fund describes its *Morningstar Sustainability Rating* calculation as :

> A two-step process. First, each fund with at least 50% of assets covered by a company-level ESG score from *Sustainalytics* receives a Morningstar Portfolio Score. The Morningstar Portfolio Score is an asset-weighted average of normalized company-level ESG scores with deductions made for controversial incidents by the issuing companies, such as environmental accidents, fraud, or discriminatory behavior.

ESG stands for Environment, Social, and Governance and incorporates the integration of all three perspectives into responsible investing strategy. I know that, but I'm not sure how the Morningstar Portfolio Score as described above relates to my mutual fund.

Whatever the score, it's important to me that the fund is 100 percent carbon-free. Not to be puritanical, but I don't want *any* of my savings to be invested in a future that cannot happen. It's not the *purity* of the position that concerns me; it's the *clarity* of the message we are sending. If and when mutual funds, institutional investors, and conglomerates get the message that we don't want to have anything to do with coal, oil, and gas, *they* will avoid coal, oil, and gas for fear of losing investors. We want to get rid of all of it!

Here's where community involvement comes in. I don't want to do this research by myself. For one thing, I don't know what I'm doing when it comes to investing. Other people who share my values know more than I do, and I would feel more comfortable buying and selling my life savings with some help—and not just from financial professionals. I want to hear from friends who care more about the world than about profits. Also, if I were to take the time to look under the hood of my own mutual fund, I would like others to benefit from what I find. I would like to talk about what I find with friends and family, and I would like to send a new sort of message to Wall Street: It's not OK to profit from the decline of human civilization, and we will isolate those who do.

Divestment is going to take some work, but it will not be as hard as finding new ways to get to work and heat our houses. So let's make this part of the overall effort.

The divestment movement on national and global levels is already in full swing. According to a Morgan-Stanley poll, 85 percent of individual investors indicate some interest in sustainability in companies they invest in; 95 percent of those investors are Millennials, which bodes well for the future. In 2015 there were 133 ESG funds available; and by 2018, the number had jumped to 350. The idea for ESG funds originated in the divestment movements against apartheid and the tobacco industry and they are a promising development toward responsible investing, but will require ongoing adjustments in values, definitions, and strategies. I'm glad there is an ESG rating on my mutual fund, even though I'm not sure what it means. I want investors and corporations to know what it means, to shun the entire fossil fuel industry, and to avoid the slightest hint of profiting from environmental destruction. I want investors and corporations to know I care. If enough people care, and show they care in an organized manner, we will create *aggregate demand* for responsible investing. To stay in business, companies will have to listen and respond accordingly.

In 2011, Hampshire College, the first college to divest from South Africa, became the first institution to divest from fossil fuel. Swarthmore College added weight to the movement in the same year by removing the coal industry from its endowment portfolio. Bill McKibben and 350.org encouraged the general public to divest from fossil fuels the following year with the *Do the Math* Tour. McKibben and others visited 300 campuses and 21 cities in North America, Asia, Europe, and Australia. Banks, trust funds, insurance companies, universities, cities, foundations, global asset managers, pension funds, faith organizations, and individual investors got the message and began selling stocks in coal, oil, natural gas, and related industries. By 2014, the amount of divested capital reached $52 billion. Mohammad Barkindo, head of the Organization of Petroleum Exporting Countries (OPEC) admitted that the "climate movement is perhaps the greatest threat to our industry going forward."

The divestment movement soared skyward in the next few years. The largest number of divesting organizations are municipalities and mission-driven institutions such as faith groups, nonprofits, foundations, health organizations, and educational institutions. But large insurance companies and pension funds also caught the fever, purged their stock holdings of carbon fuel industries, and became the largest total dollar divestors in the movement. Carbon-free investments represent 60 percent of new divestment commitments made over the past three years. In a publication from October 2018, Goldman Sachs stated, "Our Global Energy team believes that the coal divestment movement has been a key driver of the coal sector 60% de-rating over the past five years."

Seventy percent of divestment dollars are from international companies and organizations including the British Medical Association, Amundi Asset Management, Caisse des Dépôts (the French public financial institution), the Rockefeller Brothers Fund, Cape Town, the World Council of Churches, Norway's Sovereign Wealth Fund, KfW Group (Germany's development bank), Stockholm University, the Tate Museums in the U.K., and Allianz Insurance.

The Catholic Church has become one of the most active and

outspoken participants of the climate movement in general and the divestment movement in particular. In a meeting with Vatican finance ministers, Pope Francis stated, "We live at a time when profits and losses seem to be more highly valued than lives and deaths, and when a company's net worth is given precedence over the infinite worth of our human family. You are here today to reflect on how to remedy this profound crisis caused by a confusion of our moral ledger with our financial ledger.... We continue along old paths because we are trapped by our faulty accounting and by the corruption of vested interests. We still reckon as profit what threatens our very survival." Catholic institutions around the world are organizing divestment coalitions as an active means of engaging in the movement against climate change.

The Carbon Tracker Initiative, an independent investment research group founded in London in 2011, is taking an entirely different approach. Rather than promoting divestment for moral or environmental reasons, Carbon Tracker is luring investors from fossil fuel industries for financial reasons. They claim that the fossil fuel industry is reaching its peak and is, therefore, a bad place to put money. The peak will come in the next few years—around 2023—after which demand for fossil fuel will decline as renewable energy takes the lead. The math is clear: there are a total of 2,795 gigatons of CO_2 locked up in fossil fuel reserves around the world—far more than needed to ruin the climate. We can burn no more than 900 gigatons to keep average global temperatures from rising over 2 degrees Centigrade. That's only ⅓ of the total in the ground. This simple arithmetic is the basis of 350.org's *"Do the Math* Program": if the world really does decide to avoid the disaster of climate change, it will have to *not use* ⅔ of the carbon fuels that are readily available for extraction. As Carbon Tracker says, the carbon fuel industry is now experiencing a *carbon bubble.* When the bubble breaks, fossil fuel companies will end up with billions of tons of *unburnable carbon* and trillions of dollars' worth of *stranded assets* (all terms coined by Carbon Tracker). Not a good place for your life savings.

Divestment from fossil fuel companies has become the fastest-growing divestment program in history. In September of 2019, over one thousand institutions had participated, and the total dollar value of divestment topped the $11 trillion mark.

100% REAL Update: November 14, 2019

The Parks and Sustainability Committee of the Louisville Metro Council met again today to consider the resolution for 100 percent renewable energy. My councilman, who is also a sponsor of the resolution, invited the Cincinnati Energy Manager, Michael Forester, to speak and answer questions from committee members. This added great credibility to the efforts of our group, The Renewable Energy Alliance of Louisville, as Cincinnati has already passed a 100 percent resolution and is making progress in its implementation. We were hoping for a vote, but the committee decided to table the resolution once again for the sake of final rewording and preparation of a financial impact statement. On the way out, my councilman asked if we should eliminate the third part of the resolution to facilitate passage in the committee and in the council as a whole. The first part calls for 100 percent renewable electricity for city operations by 2030 and the second part for 100 percent renewable for all city operations (including transportation, heating, etc.) by 2035. The third part calls for 100 percent renewable energy for everything for the entire Louisville community by 2040. My councilman thinks this may be beyond the reach of the metro government and beyond the vote of some council members. I want to keep it in.

Meanwhile: November 16, 2019

Bishop Desmond Tutu of South Africa calls for an apartheid-era style boycott against the fossil fuel industry. He urges investors to divest of stocks in companies selling coal, oil, and gas, but he does not suggest a boycott on the consumption of their products.

8

Food

We get our food by way of tractors, fertilizers, trucks, refrigeration, and packaging.

We eat, drink, and breathe coal, oil, and natural gas.

It hasn't always been this way. Food was around for a long time before fossil carbon. But in the last century, humans discovered a way to use cheap fossil fuel to make artificial nitrogen and produce vast quantities of corn, rice, soybeans, and wheat. Billions of hungry people who would have starved were able to eat, thanks to billions of tons of nitrogen fertilizer produced by billions of tons of carbon fuel. Energy-intensive artificial fertilizer production (a method of extracting nitrogen out of the air by dumping carbon [CO_2] back into the air) began in Germany as a shortcut through the natural nitrogen cycle, but so much carbon was dumped into the air to produce it that the planetary atmosphere changed.

Nitrogen is everywhere, yet scarce. Nearly four-fifths of the air you are breathing right now is nitrogen gas, N_2. Plants and animals need nitrogen to live but cannot use it in its gaseous form, no matter how plentiful it may be. The two atoms in a molecule of nitrogen gas are so tightly bonded together that plant and animal cells cannot pry them apart. The only cells capable of *fixing* nitrogen (slicing the atoms apart and combining them with hydrogen to make ammonia, NH_3) are bacteria: nitrogen-fixing bacteria. In the form of ammonia, plants can absorb nitrogen and make protein.

For the last several hundred million years, all plant, animal, and human life on Earth has depended on nitrogen-fixing bacteria. This changed one day in the early 1900s, when Fritz Haber, a German chemist of Jewish-turned-Lutheran heritage, showed up on the

133

scene. Haber developed the energy-intensive process whereby hydrogen from natural gas (CH_4) was combined with atmospheric nitrogen gas (N_2) to produce ammonia (NH_3), a form of nitrogen that plants can absorb directly without depending on soil bacteria. The process proved extremely effective and extremely important for German agriculture during the First World War, as the British navy kept supplies of Chilean guano (a naturally produced fertilizer from bird droppings) from reaching German ports. Haber was a hero for the home team. But his great rise to patriotic fame came a little while later when he developed poison gas (chlorine) as a military weapon. Haber not only produced the poison gas, but he also supervised the first-ever poison gas attack on the western front in April of 1915. His young wife, Clara, also a chemist (and the first German woman to be awarded a doctorate in chemistry), apparently did not approve of her husband's practical application of the chemical sciences. She was a pacifist. When Haber came home shortly after the world premier of chemical warfare, she borrowed his service revolver, walked out the back door, and shot herself.

After the war Haber went on to a brilliant career in chemistry, receiving the Noble Prize in 1918 for the invention of nitrogen fertilizer. He served as director of the Kaiser Wilhelm Institute until 1933 when, despite his many sacrifices for the fatherland, he was forced out by the Nazis.

Plants cannot grow without nitrogen. I have learned this firsthand. When I planted a garden many years ago in an old, worn-out tobacco patch, I used nitrogenous compost or manure to feed plants. Where I put it, plants grew; where I did not, they did not. Heavy nitrogen feeders like corn turned light green or yellow until they got their scoop of the good stuff. A day or two later they turned dark green and started growing upward. Plants need nitrogen. Fritz Haber made compost and manure unnecessary by bypassing the nitrogen cycle altogether. Now, you don't need to get nitrogen from the soil; you can get it in a plastic bag. With enough natural gas, you can take nitrogen out of the air, put it in a bag, and feed billions of people without worrying about nitrogen-fixing bacteria in the ground. You don't really need soil at all. Soil is useful for holding plants upright, but you can do without it as long as you have nitrogen. Or phosphorus, or potassium. You can get them in a bag, too.

The natural forms of nitrogen, phosphorus, and potassium depend on plant decomposition in the soil. Each nutrient is absorbed by plants and animals while they live and returned to the soil when they die. There is no need to add fertility to the soil. Nitrogen is a little different from the others in that it gradually escapes from the soil in gaseous form and returns to the air. The natural cycle depends on bacteria constantly turning atmospheric N_2 back into NH_3 and fixing it in the soil, ready for plants to absorb. So, what happens when you artificially take billions of tons of nitrogen directly out of the atmosphere and spread it on the ground? About half of it goes into the stalks and leaves of corn, wheat, and soybeans. The other half runs off the ground into streams and rivers, feeding algae blooms that suck the oxygen out of the water, killing fish and other aquatic animals in the streams, and then killing saltwater species as de-oxygenated water empties into the sea. The 8,000 square-mile dead zone at the mouth of the Mississippi River is a direct consequence of artificial fertilizer applications in the American Midwest. All that nitrogen run-off can't complete its natural cycle back to the air and keeps on fertilizing algae all the way to the Gulf of Mexico.

But this book is about carbon, not nitrogen. What is the connection? The connection is the harnessing of carbon on a planetary scale that makes possible the harnessing of nitrogen on a planetary scale. It takes huge quantities of carbonaceous natural gas (CH_4) to produce all those millions of tons of nitrogen fertilizer, and it takes millions of gallons of carbonaceous petroleum (C_8H_{18}, or octane, more-or-less) to till the soil, apply the fertilizer, and transport the product to market. More millions of tons of carbonaceous coal (just plain old C, for the most part) or gas are required to generate electricity for drying grain, refrigeration, packaging, etc. Harnessing carbon makes harnessing nitrogen possible, which makes the harnessing of more carbon necessary. They work together. You can't have one without the other. You can't have a dead zone in the Gulf of Mexico without an oversupply of spent carbon fuel (CO_2) in the atmosphere. You can't have 7 billion people eating food on a planet this size without enormous consumption of both fossil fuel and nitrogen fertilizer.

Or can you?

Nearly fifty years ago I read a book called *Diet for a Small Planet,* by Frances Moore Lappé. Knowing at that moment in my young life that there was something fundamentally impractical about the American way of life, I began trying, with friends, to find what we would now call a *sustainable* way to live. Having opted out of the mainstream of the society in which I was raised, I was already living on the land. Lappé's book provided a window into a new world where billions of people ate well and lived well on the home planet. Animals, forests, deserts, and tundra had the room they needed. Food was plentiful enough to feed everyone. The water was clean. The air was clean. Nutrients came into the soil at the rate they went out of the soil. Soil formed at the rate it eroded. The key to unlocking this world was a careful use of nitrogen, more specifically *protein*: the form nitrogen takes to become useful to a living body. Nitrogen is the keystone element in the proteins that make up muscles, sinews, nerves, skin, organs, etc., in all living organisms. Your body is made of protein. To grow, or to repair body tissues as you move about, you need protein in your diet every day. You need bacteria in the soil turning nitrogen into plant protein. When you stray away from soil bacteria by producing artificial nitrogen—and thus protein—on a planetary scale, you run into serious ecological imbalances on a planetary scale.

If you resort to the Haber process to feed billions of people, there are too many people.

…Unless there is a different way to feed people.

Americans, and now hundreds of millions of other people in the developing world, get most of their protein from meat. We plant seeds, apply fertilizer, and harvest billions of tons of high-protein grain, but we don't eat it. We feed it to chickens, hogs, and cattle. Our protein comes from animal products. This protein is very high quality—we live high on the hog. The problem is that animal protein is inefficient. It takes five pounds of plant protein to make one pound of chicken protein, eight pounds to make one pound of hog protein, and twenty-one pounds to make a single pound of beef protein. If we were to eat the plant protein directly, there would be more to go around—a lot more. In fact, most people in most parts of the world get most of their protein from plants. The meat-eaters—those in the minority sector of the world population able to afford animal protein *every day*—are taking up most of the agricultural space the planet has to offer, and they are creating dead zones and climate change in the process. To share this small planet equitably, we need to eat plants directly. Doing so would save a lot of killing, too.

But who wants to eat cow food? Ground corn and soybeans just don't have the culinary zing of a medium-rare rib-eye. This is where the *Diet* part of Lappé's book comes in. A plant-based diet is not about eliminating meat; it's about learning new ways to eat plants. The immediate problem (besides learning new recipes) is getting enough protein from lower quality protein sources. What makes animal protein high quality is that it is usually a complete protein, meaning it has all the *amino acids* your body needs. Amino acids are nitrogen-carrying molecules that are like the bricks of which a building is built. How amino acids are stacked together determines whether the building (the protein) becomes an arm or a leg or a membrane in the pancreas. (DNA is the blueprint that dictates how amino acids are assembled.) There are twenty-two kinds of amino acids with names like *leucine*, *lysine*, and *tryptophan*. Your body needs all twenty-two at hand when it comes time to build more you: more muscles, sinews, nerves, skin, hair, fingernails, and organs. If there are enough of the first twenty-one amino acids available but only half enough of the twenty-second, your body can make only half as much total protein. It has to have all twenty-two *at the same meal* to make use of any of them. That's why meat is a good source of protein. All twenty-two amino acids are there every time. If you want to get enough protein from plants, you have to give some thought to the concept of *protein combinations*. With the right combinations of two or more amino acid sources, you get more high-quality protein out of the mix than is available in each source separately. There's more protein in beans *and* rice than there is in either beans *or* rice.

If, at a meal, you eat one type of plant that is low in certain essential amino acids—say a grain like corn, wheat, or rice—but also at the same meal eat another type of plant that is high in the amino acids lacking in grain—say pinto beans or black-eyed peas—the two sources of amino acids *complement* each other. The beans are high in those the corn is low in, and the corn is high in those the beans are low in. The result is that you get much more high-quality protein from the combination than you would get from either eaten separately—much more. The whole is more than the sum of its parts. With a little knowledge of which foods are high in which amino acids and which low in others, you can come up with a wide variety of protein combinations that can feed a small planet, without causing dead zones or climate change.

It's not hard. I've done it. I've built a house, dug a road, brought in a crop or two from the field, and walked a few miles, all on plant protein. Never missed meat. I ate a little now and again when it was served to me, but I never missed it when it was not. I've never been a foodie. I don't cook much. (My family won't let me.) I like to eat, but I don't think much about diet. I just know the basics, and the people I love and live with do, too: put some lentils in with the rice, a little soy flour in with the bread dough. Pretty simple, really. Protein can go a long way if we don't divert it to animal feed.

Meat is not necessary for protein. You can get all the protein you need from plants. You can eat no meat at all and be strong and healthy. Or, you can eat a little meat now and again. Whatever. But you do not need to eat it every day. If you eat meat every day you are contributing to dead zones, hunger, deforestation, malnutrition, and global warming. Not directly—you can't see what you are doing from the dinner table—but you are doing it.

But is it practical, you may wonder, for people around the world to be constantly checking amino acid lists every time they plan a meal or plant the seeds that become the meal?

I have asked myself this question. Familiarity with how amino acids work is not general knowledge within the global farming population. Yet I have found that the plants that complement each other on the table are often the same plants that complement each other in the field. The best protein combinations are grains (corn, wheat, rice, etc.) and legumes (beans and lentils). Grains are nitrogen feeders—they won't grow without nitrogen. Legumes are nitrogen producers—they grow symbiotically with nitrogen-fixing bacteria. So, if you plant grains and beans together—in alternating rows or alternating years—the grains will have nitrogen left over from the legumes. People all over the world have known this for centuries. American Indians traditionally grow and eat corn, beans, and squash together, a combination known as *The Three Sisters*. Beans provide nitrogen for corn; corn provides a stalk for beans to grow upon; squash vines cover the ground between stalks, shading weeds, and keeping the soil cool. American Indians did not have to read books about bacteria and amino acids to know how to grow and eat the food they needed to be healthy.

Without an Iroquois grandmother to help me figure it out, I've been trying to perfect a Three Sisters garden patch for many years. First, I just planted several rows of corn and stuck some bean and squash seeds in among the rows. The corn did fine (with compost), but the beans vines were too short and never grew up the stalks. The squash didn't have enough sun. Later, I learned to plant *pole beans*, which have longer vines. But the beans grew faster than the corn and had no stalk to climb on. So I switched back to *bush beans*—the shorter vines—and planted them separately, rotating corn and beans every year. For the squash, I learned to leave out a cornrow in the middle of the patch, so big squash leaves near the roots would have plenty of open sun and outer vines could still crawl around and cover the ground between corn stalks. This all worked pretty well for several years, but I always wondered, why can't I get these three crops to grow together the way the Indians do?

The problem was the corn. Not the corn itself—the time and

space dimensions surrounding the corn. I was planting corn seeds 5–6 inches apart in thick rows three feet apart. This is the way my people have always planted corn. Then I was trying to cram the beans and squash into the same space at the same time. Corn does have to be planted fairly densely—it's wind-pollinated: each ear needs lots of other ears nearby to complete its pollination, filling out all the kernels. But I was planting it *too* densely. So, instead of planting in rows, I have begun planting corn in *hills* four feet by four feet apart. (A "hill" is not really a hill; it's just a little spot in the garden with several seeds planted in a circle.) Then, after the corn has had a chance to grow a bit, I plant the pole beans and then, a while later, the squash. Each has its own space and its own time for harvest. They help each other grow and complement each other's amino acids at the dinner table. Through science, we now have a sophisticated understanding of an ecological interrelationship American Indians have known about for a thousand years.

I should add here that growing what you eat is only half the solution. The other half is eating what you grow—often the greater challenge. You may picture the Three Sisters as ears of golden yellow sweet corn, fresh Blue Lake green beans, and yellow summer squash. That's part of the picture, but not all of it. Most of the corn is a dent variety left on the stalk until it is dry enough to grind for cornmeal; most of the beans are dry pintos, black beans, and black-eyed peas; and most of the squash is butternut, a winter variety suitable for storage. Sweet corn on the cob, green beans, and yellow squash are all good in their season, but if you want to eat in the wintertime what you grow in the summertime, you will have to find a way to store food. Sweet corn, green beans, and summer squash all require freezing or canning for storage. Dent corn, dry beans, and winter squash are just left to dry. They last through the winter (and into the next year) without energy input. No freezing, refrigeration, or processing of any kind is required, which means no fossil fuel is used.

Growing food organically means you do not use chemical fertilizers, herbicides, or insecticides. But what do you use? As you harvest from the land you have to give something back to the land.

What? Leaves and grass clippings work well. I used to fire up the rototiller every spring, till the soil several times before planting, and then till between rows as plants sprouted and reached into the sunshine. That aerated the soil and kept the weeds back. But I don't plow or till anymore. I use leaves and grass. I spread them several inches deep in the fall and then again after plants emerge in the spring. It's a lot of work, but saves a lot of other kinds of work—hoeing, weeding, and watering. The mulch cover (dead leaves and grass) is full of phosphorus, potassium, and other minerals. It keeps weeds from growing between rows, cools the soil, and keeps the ground from drying out. As the mulch decomposes it feeds nitrogen-fixing bacteria in the soil. The soil has been building up organic matter for so long now I no longer worry about nitrogen. I don't need to put any in the soil; it's already there. And there's plenty more in the air just above the ground.

I wish this method of growing food on a small scale without fossil fuel were applicable everywhere. It's not. Other places don't have the leaves and grass we have in Kentucky. Drier climates don't grow as many tree leaves or as much grass. Larger, commercial-scale gardens might not be able to keep enough ground covered in permanent mulch. But then again, drier climates don't have as many weeds, and commercial gardens will find efficiencies of scale unavailable on a family garden. A new generation of electric machinery suitable for solar power is just around the corner. I just bought a small electric, solar-powered tractor-mower. Every situation is different, but within natural carbon and nitrogen cycles, there are a number of ways to grow all the high energy, high protein food needed. There is no room on this small planet for dead zones and climate chaos. We must learn to eat without pumping excess carbon into the air and dumping excess nitrogen onto the ground.

In researching this chapter, I came across another book: *Diet for a Hot Planet,* by Francis Lappé's daughter, Anna Lappé. *Hot* picks up where *Small* leaves off. The climate emergency is not just due to cars, electricity, and space heating—it's caused by agriculture, too. Modern agriculture is responsible for approximately a third of the world's greenhouse gases—that's more than the total emissions from the transportation sector. The meat industry is responsible for 18 percent of total greenhouse gas emissions. Half of the Iowa corn crop does not feed people or even feed animals; it goes to make ethanol fuel. Every year, about 72 billion land animals are slaughtered for human food. That bothers me. I don't like to kill animals for my food. The carbon boycott must encompass the food that contributes to climate change.

The mix of greenhouse gases from agriculture is different from other sectors. The main difference is methane. Methane (natural gas) leaks from gas wells, fracking operations, and landfills, but most of it comes from agriculture: from cows and wetland rice production. Methane (CH_4) is both a fossil fuel and a greenhouse gas. Unlike a carbon dioxide molecule (CO_2), a methane molecule is not yet oxidized. When methane *is* oxidized (burned), the CH_4 becomes CO_2 and H_2O plus energy. Methane can be burned to heat houses, make fertilizer, make electricity, or dry grain. But before methane is burned it is a greenhouse gas because, like carbon dioxide, it traps heat in the Earth's atmosphere. There is not as much methane in the atmosphere as carbon dioxide, and it does not remain in the atmosphere as long (it naturally breaks down to CO_2 after a few years), but it is a much more potent greenhouse gas while it is in the atmosphere—23 times more potent. Over a hundred years, a methane molecule will trap 23 times more heat than a carbon dioxide molecule.

Twenty-three is, therefore, the *carbon dioxide equivalent* of methane gas. But methane is far more dangerous to climate stability than this suggests. Because it breaks down fairly rapidly, most of the climate-busting effects of methane happen in the first few years of the hundred-year timeframe the carbon dioxide equivalent is based on. (The immediate carbon equivalent is closer to 100.) A large methane burst into the atmosphere can quickly spike greenhouse warming that triggers far more drastic and irreversible feedback loops elsewhere in the climate system. A sudden rise in methane levels can, for instance, warm the climate enough over a short time to melt tundra soils, releasing vast quantities of frozen carbon dioxide (and frozen methane). This additional greenhouse gas heats the atmosphere more, which releases more frozen gases, which causes more warming, and so on. The cycle is self-perpetuating. Once the climate is trapped in a feedback loop such as this, it often becomes irreversible. In fact, the real long-range danger of continued carbon emissions, whether CH_4 or CO_2, is not so much their immediate impact, but the triggering effects have on more consequential natural feedback loops. Once the trigger is pulled, feedback loops feed themselves and cannot be stopped. There is a lot of evidence that most of the mass extinctions in the Earth's past have been caused by sudden climate changes and considerable evidence suggests that sudden climate changes are triggered by spikes in atmospheric methane.

Much happened between the publication of *Diet for a Small Planet* and *Diet for a Hot Planet*. Back in the 70s when *Diet for a Small Planet* came out, the Earth was growing small and we were worried about population growth and feeding the world; now, with *Diet for a Hot Planet*, the Earth is growing hot and we are worried about the climate. It is interesting that since *Small* was published in 1971, the "solution" to population growth and the world food supply has not been amino acid combinations in plant proteins; the answer has been the *Green Revolution*: a massive worldwide shift to more industrial fertilizers and fossil fuels, the very things that make the planet *Hot*. Nitrogen fertilizer is just too good at growing lots of quick protein, and meat is just too tasty to give up. We have been too hungry and too carnivorous to listen to Frances; now we have to—*have to*—listen to Anna ... and then re-read Frances. We have to start combining plant proteins and we have to stop eating food reliant on fossil fuels. That is how we will fight climate change and feed the world, at the same time.

Mostly.

- We have to stop eating meat. Mostly.
- We have to stop shortcutting the nitrogen cycle, mostly.
- We have to stop creating dead zones, completely.

- We have to stop using fossil fuel for agriculture. Completely.
- We have to use more human energy, more human employment, and more human intelligence to produce food.
- We have to stop buying food that puts carbon into the air and nitrogen into the Gulf of Mexico.

Just like planet Earth, a lot has happened to me between the publication of *Diet for a Small Planet* and *Diet for a Hot Planet*. I'm fifty years older, for one thing. I'm still pretty good at growing food and eating what I grow, but I have come to enjoy a hamburger and beer from time to time. I like to eat out. I admire people who never eat meat or animal products, but I don't expect everyone in the world to eat only plants or grow their own food. More people should grow food on a smaller scale, feeding themselves, and feeding others, for a living. More people should be growing more food, more intensively, more carefully, more sustainably, and those who do not grow their own food can support caring, sustainable growers by buying what they produce. There are plenty of people out there looking for something useful to do, and many of them would enjoy living and working on the land. Vote with your fork. Encourage smaller-scale food production by buying it. Discourage industrial-scale production by not buying it.

The challenge is in distinguishing between the two—what differentiates good food from bad? Organic food is grown without fertilizers and pesticides, so that's a good starting point. But I would not ban artificial fertilizers for all time; there may be ways of using them within natural cycles. I *would* ban dead zones for all time, but we should keep minds open to new ways of sustainably boosting agricultural production. There is always a trade-off between purity and openness.

Buying locally grown food at farmer's markets is also good. New methods of sustainable agriculture are most likely to emerge first from small-scale producers. Let's encourage them. But there is no set formula for "doing it right." The question of what food is best to buy should always remain an open question. The only real rule of thumb is awareness. Talk to farmers at the market and read labels at the grocery store. Read *through* the labels. Get to know what *the terms natural, grass-fed,* and *certified humane* really mean. Get to know what *organic certification* entails. Get to know the people who grow what you buy. Buy food in community with friends at a food co-op. Know where your food dollars are going; they are your signal to the greater economy. Your dollars are your vote. Make how you buy food part of the carbon boycott. Do it with other people.

And maybe, just maybe, try planting a row of pinto beans.

Organic food, at present, is more expensive than industrial food. That creates another challenge: not everyone can afford it. Purchasing organic goods is a luxury of the comfortable. Awareness of this undeniable truth should guide community action toward achieving a sustainable food supply. Every time you buy something that someone else cannot afford, you create social tension. But, as in the case of rooftop solar installations, the social divide is not a reason to avoid sustainable adaptation. It can't be. Solving two long-range problems simultaneously is rarely practical. Social inequality should not be an excuse for unsustainability. In the case of solar, the fairly wealthy early adapters created an economy of scale in solar panel production by buying panels when they were very expensive. The more they bought, the cheaper the panels became, by a factor of 5 or 6. Now, with the solar revolution in full swing, more moderate-income families (and utilities, municipalities, and industries) can afford to install solar. The dynamic will not be exactly the same with organic food, but something like it has already begun with the onset of large-scale organic production. And there may be unforeseen factors in future food prices. With the possibilities of carbon taxes, fuel embargoes, and fertilizer shortages in the coming years, organic food may become cheaper than industrial food. If and when that happens, we will be glad that early adapters created locally-based organic food production with their available dollars.

There is something else about *Small* and *Hot: us*—you and me. We're jumping up and down about climate change these days—about *hot*—but we didn't even know it was a concern fifty years ago. Climate change didn't exist fifty years ago. Now, it's all the rage. Fifty years ago we were jumping up and down about population, resource depletion, and air pollution: the same people for the most part, but different issues. What does this say?

It says one of two things: either all the issues we are concerned about are all really one big single issue or, we are people who just have to have an issue to jump up and down about, no matter what the current issue might be. Either there is a single, fundamental, unifying factor behind population, resource depletion, air pollution, and climate change, or there are people like us in the world who just can't be happy. We jumpers complain no matter what. It's one way or the other.

The truth of the matter lies in where you are looking *from*.

From the inside, *we* are the people who care. We care about other people, other nations, and other forms of life. We're likely to protest warfare, social inequality, and racial discrimination. We don't just want a "better world"; we want survival. We want justice and we want a chance for life to live in an over-industrialized society. We want the planet to survive. Some of us suspect that the nation-state is obsolete—that there is no world in a world of zero-sum nationalism.

But from the outside—and this is important for the real-world effectiveness of what we are trying to do—from the outside, we are the vilified other: the ones who don't know what we have, don't appreciate the good things, and don't respect tradition. We are the people always putting America down. One day the planet is too small for us; the next day it's too hot. And we're probably all on welfare, too!

From that perspective *we* are *them*.

It's important to know this because we're not going to get what *we* want. And *they* (the other *they*) are not going to keep *us* from getting what we want. There are no absolutes. We will end up together—with that part of ourselves that does not cancel out the other.

There are no enemies.

Meanwhile: November 26, 2019

A United Nations Annual Report states that global emissions of carbon dioxide, methane, and other greenhouse gasses have continued to increase over the last decade. The increase is driving more frequent and severe storms, droughts, heatwaves, and other extreme weather. Countries are asked to ban new coal-fired power plants and gasoline cars, expand mass transit, and require all new buildings to be entirely electric.

9

A Tale of Two Cities

Louisville and Cincinnati

If you are actively striving to achieve 100 percent renewable energy in your local city, county, or state, you are likely to end up somewhere between Louisville and Cincinnati. The following account is presented less as a comparison between cities than as an outline of obstacles you may encounter along the way.

Resolutions for 100 percent renewable energy were introduced to both Louisville and Cincinnati in September of 2018 as part of a nationwide and worldwide effort by 350.org, the Sierra Club, and other organizations. Cincinnati passed its version within three months and is now well on the way to achieving its goals. As reported in updates throughout this book, the 100% Renewable Energy Alliance of Louisville (100% REAL) is presenting the following three-part resolution to the Louisville Metro Council:

100% renewable *electricity* for all city operations by 2030
100% renewable *all forms of energy* for city operations by 2035
100% renewable energy for the entire Louisville community by 2040

The council assigned the resolution to a committee, where it died in March of 2019. It was re-introduced by a new sponsor (my councilman) in August of 2019 and reassigned to the same committee (Parks and Sustainability), where a series of hearings have been held in the fall of 2019 with presentations by four separate interested parties: the city administration (the mayor's office), the Renewable Energy Alliance of Louisville (us), Louisville Gas and Electric (our local fossil fuel monopoly), and the director of the renewable energy program in Cincinnati. Attendance by committee members has been spotty, and enthusiasm understated, though there was considerable interest at the last hearing on the Cincinnati plan. The resolution has been tabled at the end of each hearing, but a committee vote is scheduled for Thursday, December 5: ten days from now. If it passes, a vote in the full Metro Council may come up as early as the following Thursday, December 12.

We have a number of things working against us here in Louisville: the state legislature, the Kentucky Public Service Commission, and our privately-owned gas and electric monopoly.

Despite the overbearing dominance of the coal industry in our state, the legislature has shown moments of enlightenment in the past. Until the beginning of 2019, we have had a good *net metering* law that allowed utility customers with solar panels to feed excess solar energy into the grid. Most solar houses generate more electricity than they need during daylight hours, but still need electricity after the sun goes down. Net metering allows them to "store" daytime excess in the grid for use at night, on a one-for-one basis. The meter runs backward during the day and forward at night. Like a bank account, you take out what you put in. If the solar array is well designed, you put in as much as you take out, achieving carbon neutrality. Even if not, you still achieve *net metering*: you pay only for the amount you use over the amount you produce. It's a great system and not all states have it. Here in Kentucky, net metering has been the legal basis for my solar installation business. Utilities are required to let me hook customer-owned solar panels to the grid, and I can assure my customers that they will get full credit for all the electricity they generate.

But the utility industry spent over $300,000 in 2019 lobbying the Kentucky General Assembly to weaken net metering. Now, utilities can pay less for electricity "stored" during the day than they charge at night. You put a dollar in the bank and take out fifty cents. There is some justice in this: solar customers should, and will in time, pay for their use of the grid. But what's more important right now? Preventing climate disaster or nickel and diming the solar industry? The overall effect of the new legislation is to discourage the transition to renewables and seriously damage the emerging solar industry in Kentucky.

It's a big step backward. The state should be creating incentives, not setting up roadblocks.

And then there's Louisville Gas and Electric, the local utility. I appreciate that LG&E provides light, warmth, refrigeration, and entertainment. They keep my computer running—the computer I am using right now—and keep my toothbrush charged up. Thank you, LG&E! I even work alongside LG&E when hooking up solar customers. They help with the documentation and send servicemen to the site to make the grid connections. No problem. I'm pulling rate-paying customers away and they're not trying to get back at me. They are people trying to make a living like everyone else.

But it was LG&E that hired those lobbyists in the legislature. They don't see my little company as a big threat, but they want to stay in control of the production of electricity in the future. They know the climate imperative is here to stay. They know solar is the future, and they know solar is cheaper in the long run, so they want to control it. They're a monopoly and that's what monopolies do. They want to bring in solar and wind for their own profit and they want to do it on their own schedule because they have millions and millions of dollars tied up in coal-fired power plants. When 100% REAL came out with our renewable energy resolution, they came out with their "80 by 50" plan. It sounds like a compromise—OK, only 80 percent instead of 100 percent, and by 2050, not by 2030, 35, and 40: almost as good. No?

No. The 80 is not 80 percent renewable energy; it's an 80 percent reduction in carbon emissions *compared to what they are emitting now*. They're emitting a lot now, with a portfolio of about 90 percent coal generation. They plan to keep burning coal for *another twenty years*, and then bring about a gradual transition to natural gas, which is *another fossil fuel!* That way they get their money's worth out the coal plants and still get to sell us gas. Makes sense (and dollars!)—from their point of view. After all, *Gas* is their middle name.

To do what we need to do, we're going to have to go outside the city limits. The city does not control its own utilities; the state does. Gas, electric, and water distribution are regulated by the three-member Kentucky Public Service Commission, appointed by the governor. One of the commissioners, Talina Mathews, recently said publicly that Kentucky, "...still seems perfectly happy with 94% of its energy needs being supplied by coal and natural gas." She sees no need to add renewable generation. "...Green kilowatt-hours? We're going to sit back and let that come to us.... Would some people say my head is in the sand? Maybe." According to her, Kentucky residents don't care "what color the kilowatt-hours are," as long as they are cheap. That's what we're up against with the Public Service Commission.

Yet we are going to have to deal with the PSC when it comes to determining *external costs* for each type of energy used to produce electricity, costs like air pollution, black lung, asthma, mercury in waterways, road maintenance in coal country, mine restoration, water, soil, and air pollution from mountain top removal, carbon pollution, and other associated health, infrastructure, and environmental costs to the public. Coal lends its own distinct color to kilowatt-hours.

An alternative to the inclusion of external costs when determining the charge consumers pay for each type of energy would be the passage of a carbon tax by the legislature: a tax that would charge energy producers directly for external costs, costs that would put fossil fuel generation out of business. Through the PSC, the public will become involved in how energy is produced and consumed and how the cost structure of each form of energy affects living conditions for present and future generations. We will be working in the near future to change who the PSC is, how it is selected, and what it is supposed to be doing.

We are going to have to deal with the Public Service Commission also when it comes to untangling LG&E's monopoly control of power generation in Louisville. We will question the whole concept of utility monopolies. And when we do, we will distinguish between electrical *production* and electrical *distribution*. Both are "natural monopolies" now. Monopolies have made sense until now because coal or gas-fired electrical production is most practical at centralized power plants, and the distribution of more than one source of electrical power to individual buildings is impractical. You wouldn't want to have three or four different sets of wiring coming into your house. The electrical grid (*distribution*) is likely, therefore, to remain a regulated natural monopoly for the foreseeable future, but renewable energy *production* (solar, wind, hydro, geothermal) is not. Renewable energy is *decentralized*; it is produced at many "distributed" locations and presents entirely new and innovative forms of electrical energy. It is not, therefore, a natural monopoly. Electrical *production* should not remain under monopoly control. We have to clarify this distinction to the Public Service Commission and persuade them to allow market access to the grid at market prices that include external costs.

In the absence of a utility monopoly on production, we can have *community solar, investor-owned solar,* or a *solar power-purchasing plan*. All will require regulation by the PSC. A community solar installation (one owned by the shareholders and used to offset their own consumption) could produce electricity using solar panels installed on warehouses, barns, parking structures, fields, and vacant lots to supply people who do not have good solar exposure on their property. This is something we could be working on as a community. An *investor-owned* facility could produce and sell solar electricity to the grid on the open market. This would be an entrepreneurial arrangement suitable for less directly involved utility customers; customers might not even know their energy was coming from this type of facility.

A solar power-purchasing plan is the route Cincinnati has taken. The city avoids all upfront costs by signing agreements with private companies to provide solar energy at a fixed price for a fixed number of years. The company has to finance the installation but enjoys a guaranteed income stream for the duration of the contract, usually twenty years or so. It is important to note that Cincinnati is free to engage in this kind of power purchase agreement because it is not constrained by a monopoly utility.

LG&E's aim to control all energy production is an attempt to maintain its monopoly status, but that status no longer applies to the resources at hand. When large, centralized coal-fired power plants were the only option, LG&E was in a position to call the shots, but times have changed. The renewable energy we seek in Louisville will never be provided by a fossil fuel monopoly.

Our sister city Cincinnati, just a hundred miles up Interstate 71, is a different story altogether. I don't know all the particulars of how the city has managed to get where it is, but it is well on the way to a renewable energy future. I was impressed by what their director said at our Parks and Sustainability meeting here in Louisville, and I am quite sure committee members were impressed as well. Until he presented Cincinnati's path to full carbon neutrality, it seemed as if all the committee members know about 100 percent renewable energy is what they have heard from us.

Cincinnati passed their 100 percent resolution on December 10, 2018, becoming the 100th U.S. city to pledge carbon neutrality by 2035. A resolution is not legally binding, but Mayor John Cranley said, " by adopting it, the city council is committing to something we're already trying to do, but going on the record." The resolution promises that "all of the City-owned and operated facilities and fleets" will transition to 100 percent clean and renewable energy sources over the next 17 years. It also pledges, "to ensure that 100 percent of the electricity consumed by residents and businesses within the city shall be generated by clean, renewable sources such as solar and wind."

The mayor added, "This serves as a mandate. We don't want to just say 'no' to coal. We want to say 'yes' to solar, and here's how to do it…. It has become clear," he went on, "that cities will lead the global effort to fight climate change, and Cincinnati is on the front lines. I am encouraged by the changes we are making, but we have a lot of work left to do."

Cincinnati is already implementing the plan. As a first big step, the city has committed to building a 25-megawatt solar array: an installation Mayor Cranley calls the largest municipal solar array in the country. This array will power a full quarter of the city's energy needs. "Cities need to take action—and that's exactly what Cincinnati is doing. We are spending money we would already spend on power to buy lower-cost renewable energy that also benefits the community." The thousand-acre solar farm, which will include more than 310,000 solar panels, will be installed 40 miles east of downtown Cincinnati in Highland County. It will keep 157 million pounds of coal in the ground every year, the carbon-reduction equivalent of removing 30,000 cars from the road or planting 2.4 million trees. The city will pay no upfront costs toward the construction of the solar farm and mandate that the project hire its workforce through a program at Cincinnati State and IBEW Local 212. The power purchase agreement stipulates that the city will purchase electrical energy at a fixed rate for 20 years. "We are fortunate in Cincinnati to have leaders who provide leadership," said the city's director of the Office of Environment and Sustainability. "I will be working to make these goals a reality. With the many partners who are stepping up to help implement the Green Cincinnati Plan, 100 percent renewable energy by 2035 is an attainable goal."

Neil Waggoner, Campaign Representative of the Ohio Sierra Club's *Beyond Coal* campaign was disappointed in Duke Energy's reluctance to cooperate. "Cincinnati's announcement is exciting but it also underscores how out of touch the local electric utility Duke is with its customers. While Cincinnatians embrace clean energy, Duke continues to try to force them to bail out old dirty coal plants, notably the Clifty Creek coal plant just across the border in Indiana that blows pollution into the Queen City every day."

"Cincinnati is a bright spot for clean energy, not only in Ohio, but among cities across the country that are leading the way to a more sustainable future," Ohio's Natural Resources Defense Council (NRDC) Energy Policy Director Daniel Sawmiller said. "Today's announcement of a significant city-led solar energy development creates a crucial economic opportunity for Ohio and sets a new bar for cities that have committed to 100 percent renewable energy across the country." Cincinnati was one of 25 cities chosen in October 2018 by the Bloomberg American Cities Climate Challenge to beat carbon-reduction goals with a two-year acceleration program. "Cincinnati was selected as a winner in the American Cities Climate Challenge because of Mayor Cranley's commitment to ambitious and impactful climate solutions—solutions which not only reduce carbon emissions but also protect public health and create jobs," Bloomberg

Philanthropies Head of Environmental Programs Antha Williams said. "This offsite renewable deal is the latest example of Cincinnati's ambition turned into achievement.... Cincinnati is showing how cities are leading the way to our clean energy future and paving the way for others in the region to follow suit."

Where we in Louisville have a dozen or two active volunteer members of 100% REAL, Cincinnati has The Greater Cincinnati Energy Alliance, a much larger professionally staffed nonprofit organization with a mission to be the leading driver of activities that reduce carbon emissions in the city and its hinterlands. Founded in 2009, the Energy Alliance was awarded a grant the following year from the U.S. Department of Energy's Better Buildings Neighborhood Program. The organization helps finance commercial solar installations through the Property Assessed Clean Energy (PACE) program and assists residential solar through its Get Efficient and Solarize programs.

Site Selection magazine named Cincinnati the country's "most sustainable city," and the blog *Triple Pundit* calls Cincinnati "one of the greenest and most innovative cities in the nation. No longer known for just chili, baseball, and the second-largest Octoberfest in the world (outside of Munich), Cincinnati is evolving into a hub for technology, sustainability, and social innovation." Joi M. Sears wrote in a recent post. "It's not that Cincinnati has more money than other Midwestern cities, it's just that those with the money are more deeply connected to the ecosystem of people and young companies with innovative ideas." The Green Cincinnati Plan includes 60 sustainability initiatives in renewable energy, transportation, and food waste. Finally, a *Triple Pundit* post says, "When it comes to the intersection of sustainability and innovation, Cincinnati is certainly thinking outside the box." The blog points to plans to use sustainability to combat poverty, prevent crime through environmental design, and leverage big data to drive change. Specifically, it touts the LEED-certified District 3 police headquarters and city decision-making based on data it collects.

Remaining active in state and municipal politics is important and should be part of any climate or environmental group's stated purpose. But I think that a grass-roots volunteer community group that concentrates on shaping aggregate energy consumption is even more important for two reasons. First, it's more fundamental. It's where carbon use happens. To get this movement right, we have to know where our energy is coming from and where it is going, and we have to live it in our own lives. Professionally staffed groups don't do that. Secondly, we need to be election proof. We need to organize and maintain a boycott of carbon fuels on the individual and community level whether or not we produce electoral majorities. The boycott can be done without government: state, local, or national. It can go on whether or not we win or lose governors, presidents, or seats in the legislature.

Let's try to win elections. We need new leadership on local, state, national, and global levels. But we vote with our dollars no matter who is in office.

Just don't buy the stuff.

Then again, those of us without a suitable roof or an extra $20,000 for a solar installation are going to have to go with community solar, renewable investor-owned solar, or a municipal power purchase plan. That takes politics. Not buying becomes a community effort.

Cincinnati proves that 100 percent renewable can happen. We can do it and you can do it. Here in Louisville, we're going to take our time and do it a little differently.

100% REAL Update: October 17, 2019

The Louisville Metro Council Committee on Parks and Sustainability met again today to consider the Resolution for 100 percent renewable. With another 100% REAL member, I spoke to the committee emphasizing that the Resolution is not an answer to the climate problem, but a question: "With all our infrastructure built around fossil fuel, how will we make the transition to renewables?" The committee heard from the mayor's office at its previous meeting and will hear from the utility company, Louisville Gas and Electric, at its next meeting. We expect a vote then or shortly thereafter.

10

The Intergovernmental Panel on Climate Change

The Intergovernmental Panel on Climate Change (IPCC) assesses scientific research related to climate change. It is not a research institution, but compiles, evaluates, and summarizes a comprehensive body of climate information from research institutions around the world, and presents options for mitigation and adaptation. It assembles what the world knows about the climate crisis in one place. By doing so, it helps governments negotiate on the international level and make informed policy decisions at all levels, but it does not recommend specific policies. Hundreds of scientists from 195 member nations volunteer time every year to assess thousands of published scientific papers on the Earth's climate. Every 3 to 5 years the IPCC issues a new comprehensive report on the current status of climate change and on where future greenhouse gas emissions are likely to lead.

The panel was created by the United Nations in 1988 and issued its first report in 1990. In 2007 it was awarded the Nobel Peace Prize (along with Al Gore) for "its efforts to build up and disseminate greater knowledge of man-made climate change, and to lay the foundations for the measures that are needed to counteract such change."

But why no recommendations? The IPCC knows more about what's happening to the Earth's climate than anyone else, so why not say what to do? Why not just tell us so we can do what needs to be done? They don't tell us what to do because of three things we believe in: science, democracy, and the existential imperative of human volition. Science is vision, not policy. It shows us what is. Policy consolidates vision to the practical. Democracy requires that we do what the majority wants, regardless of vision and propriety. Scientists are a minority; if the rest of us deny what they show to be true, so be it. We go with majority rule, for better or worse. And we believe that humanity exists in a perennial state of choice or does not exist at all. Truth is not given us in certain terms—we determine what we think is true; we act; and we live with the actions we take. Without choice, there would be no awareness of life and nothing to live for.

The findings of the IPCC are based on science: the best, most comprehensive, complete, unreduced, and accurate science available. At this moment, the IPCC is the eyesight of humanity. Through its process, we know what is happening. Few pay attention, but we know. IPCC reports always seem to fit in around the edges of the news. Personalities are always at the center of the news, not science or climate; but we know. Everybody knows at some level that we have to do something quickly. How and if we respond produces what we deserve.

IPCC reports are unique in their global perspective. They are not one nation's take on what to do about its own national atmosphere. They are the world looking at itself. To look as a world is to see anew. To look as a world is to see unity in the dangers we saw before. From this standpoint, we may act appropriately.

> When two or more problems have the same root;
> They have the same solution.

> Discovering unity in the atmosphere makes war silly.

IPCC scientists are chosen as experts in their fields, taking into account their scientific, technical, and economic views. Gender and geographical balance are important factors in determining who participates. Many scientists without previous experience with the panel are chosen to avoid established biases. Their work consists mainly of reading and evaluating thousands of peer-reviewed articles in scientific and technical journals. Experts from industry and non-government organizations are invited to participate in the assessment. Draft assessments, once written by IPCC scientists, are subject to reviews for accuracy and completeness by hundreds of other readers in a wide variety of scientific fields.

I'm going to take a chance here and go into a little more detail on the IPCC's 2018 special report "Global Warming of 1.5°C," which is the one by 91 scientists from 40 countries, reviewing 6000 studies on climate change, trusting that you can appreciate the significance of what these findings reveal about just where we are in this climate crisis. I am reasonably sure you are already convinced we should stop burning coal, oil, and natural gas as soon as possible, but this study gives more detail on why that is important now. How we choose to act in the 2020s will have a great deal to do with how people live in the remaining eighty years of this century and whether people live at all in the next.

Already, this is new. Whoever cared about how people will live 50 years in the future?

The 2018 U.N. Intergovernmental Panel on Climate Change assessment emphasizes the difference between 1.5° C global warming and 2.0° global warming—only half a degree. Not much on the thermometer—but a big difference on the Earth. Much more climate change is coming no matter what we do: the question here is, "How bad will it be?" With 1.5°, we will get by, more or less. With 2.0°, things will be much worse.

Here's where we stand: The preindustrial baseline for this study (and almost all others) is the period from about 10,000 BCE up until 1880. Carbon dioxide concentrations throughout this 100-century period remained close to 280 parts per million, and average global temperatures remained steady, with some slow-paced variations. This constitutes the *pre-industrial* climate, the period known geologically as the *Holocene*. Since 1880, carbon dioxide concentrations have grown from 280 ppm to about 417 ppm (nearly half again as much CO_2 in the air), and average global temperatures have risen by about 1.0° Centigrade. That is what has happened up to 2020. Warming of 1.5° C means another 0.5 degrees beyond where we are now, and 2.0° means another 1.0° of warming. Doesn't sound like much.

No matter what we do—even if we stop all new carbon emissions tomorrow morning—global temperatures will keep rising over the next few decades, reaching around 1.5° between 2030 and 2052. But—and this is the good news—if we stop emissions now, or very soon, global warming will not go *beyond* 1.5°. We can still save this thing.

Here, in more detail, are some of the findings of "Global Warming of 1.5°C."

. . . .

Warming greater than the global annual average is being experienced in many seasons and land regions. In fact, warming, which is generally higher over land than over the ocean, is two to three times higher in the Arctic.

. . . .

Greenhouse emissions *from the past* are unlikely to increase global temperature more than .5° C in the future. (The damage we have done already is limited. This is good news.)

. . . .

Global warming impacts on natural and human systems have already been observed. Many land and ocean ecosystems and some of the services they provide have already changed due to global warming.

. . . .

Global mean sea level rise by 2100 for 1.5°C of global warming would be 0.1 m less than it would be for a global warming of 2°C. This reduction in sea-level rise implies that up to 10 million fewer people would be exposed to related risks. (That's a biggie.)

. . . .

Sea level rise will continue beyond 2100 even if global warming is limited to 1.5°C in the twenty-first century. Marine ice sheet instability in Antarctica and/or irreversible loss of the Greenland ice sheet could result in a multi-meter rise in sea level over hundreds to thousands of years. These instabilities could be triggered at around 1.5°C to 2°C.

. . . .

To limit warming to 1.5° C we will have to reduce carbon emissions by 45 percent by 2030. (That's ten years from now.)

. . . .

To keep warming to 1.5° C we will have to reduce carbon emissions by 100 percent by 2050. (No oil, no coal, no gas—thirty years.)

. . . .

Pathways reflecting current nationally stated mitigation ambition until 2030 are broadly consistent with cost-effective pathways that result in a global warming of about 3°C by 2100, with warming continuing afterward. (This is a way biggie: even if governments *actually do* what they say they will do, temperatures will go well above 1.5°—or even above 2.0°. Governments don't get it! This is much bigger than they think!)

. . . .

Reversing warming after an overshoot of 2.0 °C or more during this century would require upscaling and deployment of CDR (carbon dioxide reduction) at rates and volumes that might not be achievable given considerable implementation challenges.

. . . .

(If we go over 1.5, we may never be able to bring temperatures back down again, even with new technologies that take CO_2 out of the air.)

. . . .

The lower the emissions in 2030, the lower the challenge in limiting global warming to 1.5°C after 2030 with no or limited overshoot. The challenges from delayed actions to reduce greenhouse gas emissions include the risks of cost escalation, lock-in in carbon-emitting infrastructure, stranded assets, and reduced flexibility in future response options in the medium to long term. (If we go over 1.5° by 2030, it's going to get a lot harder and a lot more expensive just to stay where we are.)

. . . .

Future climate-related risks depend on the rate, peak, and duration of warming. In the aggregate, these are larger if global warming exceeds 1.5°C before returning to that level by 2100 than if global warming gradually stabilizes at 1.5°C, especially if the peak temperature is high (e.g., about 2°C). Some impacts may be long-lasting or irreversible, such as the loss of some ecosystems. (This is an interesting "detail" that people may feel for decades: if we go above 1.5°, to say around 2.0°, and then come back down again to 1.5° by the end of the century, the effect will be worse than if we never exceeded 1.5°—a few more ecosystems worse.)

· · · · · · · · · · · ·

Limiting global warming to 1.5°C rather than 2°C is projected to prevent the thawing over centuries of a permafrost area in the range of 1.5 to 2.5 million km². (This is the real biggie—the potential triggering of a catastrophic feedback loop. Melting permafrost would release more carbon dioxide and methane into the air, further warming the planet, melting the permafrost, and so on. This is how most mass extinctions begin. If we can avoid exceeding 1.5° warming, we might avoid triggering this feedback loop.)

· · · · · · · · · · · ·

Limiting global warming to 1.5°C is projected to reduce risks to marine biodiversity, fisheries, and ecosystems, and their functions and services to humans, as illustrated by recent changes to Arctic sea ice and warm-water coral reef ecosystems. Coral reefs, for example, are projected to decline by a further 70–90 percent at 1.5°C with larger losses (>99 percent) at 2.0°C. The risk of irreversible loss of many marine and coastal ecosystems increases with global warming, especially at 2°C or more.

· · · · · · · · · · · ·

Climate-related risks to health, livelihoods, food security, water supply, human security, and economic growth are projected to increase with global warming of 1.5°C and increase further with 2°C.

· · · · · · · · · · · ·

Limiting warming to 1.5°C compared with 2°C is projected to result in smaller net reductions in yields of maize, rice, wheat, and potentially other cereal crops, particularly in sub-Saharan Africa, Southeast Asia, and Central and South America. The CO_2-dependent nutritional quality of rice and wheat could be minimized as well. Limiting global warming to 1.5°C compared to 2°C may reduce the proportion of the world population exposed to a climate change-induced increase in water stress by up to 50 percent.

· · · · · · · · · · · ·

Estimates of the global emissions outcome of current nationally stated mitigation ambitions as submitted under the Paris Agreement would lead to global greenhouse gas emissions in 2030 of 52–58
$GtCO_2eq$ per year (52–58 billion tons of carbon dioxide equivalents
per year). Pathways reflecting these ambitions would not limit global
warming to 1.5°C, even if supplemented by very challenging increases
in the scale and ambition of emissions reductions after 2030. (Paris is
way not enough.)

The 2.0° limit was the gold standard for global warming up until
2018. It should be 1.5°. But emissions are increasing, not decreasing. We
are getting farther and farther from the possibility of staying under the
increased limit of 2.0°. "Political reality" is nowhere near 1.5°. But in a
democracy, "political reality" is a creation of the people. In an economy—democratic or otherwise—the economic reality is a creation of the
consumer. Forty-five percent fewer emissions by 2030? Why not? Who's
going to buy the rest of all that carbon?

In 2019 the IPCC came out with the special reports "Climate and
Land" and "The Ocean and Cryosphere in a Changing Climate." Here
are a few more facts from those reports.

· · · · · · · · · · · · ·

Agriculture, forestry, and other land-use activities accounted
for around 13 percent of carbon dioxide (CO_2), 44 percent of
methane (CH_4), and 82 percent of nitrous oxide (N_2O) emissions
from human activities globally during 2007–2016. If emissions
associated with pre- and post-production activities in the global
food system are included, the emissions are estimated to be 21–37
percent of total net anthropogenic GHG emissions. (Food is a huge
part of the Green House Gas climate picture.)

· · · · · · · · · · · · ·

Asia and Africa are projected to have the highest number of people
vulnerable to increased desertification. North America, South
America, the Mediterranean, southern Africa, and central Asia
may be increasingly affected by wildfire. The tropics and subtropics
are projected to be most vulnerable to crop yield decline. Land
degradation resulting from the combination of sea-level rise
and more intense cyclones is projected to jeopardize lives and

livelihoods in cyclone-prone areas. Within populations, women, the very young, the elderly, and the poor are most at risk.

．．．．．．．．．．．．．

During 2010–2016, global food loss and waste contributed 8–10 percent of total anthropogenic GHG emissions. Currently, 25–30 percent of total food produced is lost or wasted.

．．．．．．．．．．．．．

Since 1993, the rate of ocean warming has more than doubled. Marine heatwaves have very likely doubled in frequency since 1982 and are increasing in intensity. By absorbing more CO_2, the ocean has undergone increasing surface acidification.

．．．．．．．．．．．．．

Increases in tropical cyclone winds and rainfall, and increases in extreme waves, combined with relative sea-level rise, exacerbate extreme sea-level events and coastal hazards.

．．．．．．．．．．．．．

Since the mid-twentieth century, the shrinking cryosphere (ice) in the Arctic and high-mountain areas has led to predominantly negative impacts on food security, water resources, water quality, livelihoods, health and well-being, infrastructure, transportation, tourism and recreation, as well as on the culture of human societies, particularly for indigenous peoples. Costs and benefits have been unequally distributed across populations and regions. Adaptation efforts have benefited from the inclusion of indigenous knowledge and local knowledge.

．．．．．．．．．．．．．

Widespread permafrost thaw is projected for this century and beyond. Projected near-surface (within 3–4 m) permafrost area shows a decrease of 24 ± 16 percent by 2100. This scenario would lead to the cumulative release of tens to hundreds of billions of tons (GtC) of permafrost carbon as CO_2 and methane into the atmosphere by 2100 with the potential to exacerbate climate change. (This is the dreaded feedback loop, a game-changer for existing life on Earth. Notice that this 2019 study assumes that warming will not be kept within 1.5°C.)

．．．．．．．．．．．．．

Extreme El Niño and La Niña events are projected to become more frequent.

. . . .

Extreme sea levels and coastal hazards will be exacerbated by projected increases in tropical cyclone intensity and precipitation. The average intensity of tropical cyclones, the proportion of Category 4 and 5 tropical cyclones, and the associated average precipitation rates are projected to increase for a 2°C global temperature rise above any baseline period.

. . . .

The sixth IPCC assessment report is due out in April of 2021.

100% REAL Update: December 2, 2019

Five people from 100% REAL met this afternoon with four members of the Louisville Office of Sustainability to discuss how to move forward with the renewable energy transition in our city. If and when our resolution passes in Metro Council (legislative branch), we will be working with these people (executive branch) on implementation. I shared some figures on rooftop solar and how much land will be needed to power city operations and the entire community. We talked about the possibility of hiring an energy manager and forming a stakeholder's council to oversee the transition.

Meanwhile: December 2, 2019

The United Nations began its Climate Conference in Madrid. At the opening plenary, U.N. Chief Antonio Guterres asked, "Do we really want to be remembered as the generation that buried its head in the sand, that fiddled while the planet burned?" The last five years have been the hottest ever recorded, he reminded the assembly. Permafrost is melting in the Arctic 70 years ahead of projections, and Antarctica is melting three times as fast as a decade ago. To prevent temperatures from rising above 1.5 degrees C, the global economy must be carbon neutral by mid-century. He praised the findings of the U.N. Intergovernmental Panel on Climate Change as "...the best available science."

11

Committing to the Boycott

I go back and forth on the urgency of the message.

Between:
"Take it easy, don't panic. Do it as you can. Let's use the time we have to do it right."
And:
"This is huge! It's happening fast—*do* panic! This is life or death and it's getting worse every day!"

What are we thinking?

What are we waiting for?

Those of you reading this in the second half of the century—in the next century—forgive us for not knowing how serious this is going to be. We know what science tells us, but we don't know what you see out the window. We don't know if there is nothing to be alarmed about or if there is everything to be alarmed about. We panic too soon or we don't panic soon enough: we have no way of knowing. Understand that we see the beginning of what looks like centuries of bad weather and sea-level rise, but these are abstractions for us. We see a tiny sliver with our eyes; the rest of the picture is what we think is true. Out in the streets, everything looks normal to us now. Cars drive by; people go shopping; neighbors live in big warm houses. It's all so normal. We cannot see what you see.

So let's go with what we do know: the climate is changing and it's because of human oxidation of carbon. We don't know how fast or how severe the changes will be, but it's pretty clear that the more carbon burnt, the worse they will be.

We also know that the transition to renewable energy will be extremely difficult and disruptive for most people. In fact, it may not be a *transition* at all. It may be a *revolution*: a thorough, rapid, all-encompassing fundamental shift from one lifestyle to another, a shift that will be resisted by those who do not understand it. That's all we have to know to get started. Now.

We should aim at transition. Don't panic. The shift to renewables may turn into revolution at some point, but the more transitional it is now the less revolutionary it will be later. I'm not opposed to revolution—the threat of climate change is worth a revolution. But I don't like the idea of it. I don't like revolution and think it can be avoided for the most part. I think if enough people—*communities* of people—figure out what changes are necessary and how to make them happen in the real world, the revolution can be avoided, or if not avoided, less severe.

The sooner we start, the less severe the weather.

The more intentional we are, the less severe the transition.

But how realistic is a carbon boycott? Will people really do it? Will *we* do it? Will we stop driving cars and heating houses if we have to? This is where a touch of revolution comes in handy—a little measure of panic. Every day we drive our cars, heat our houses, and run our refrigerators, we damage the only known biosphere in the universe. We're damaging ourselves, our country, our grandchildren, and life itself. The ice cap is melting. We are changing the Earth's atmosphere in ways that cause mass extinctions. We're destroying that which has been given us in trust. The house is on fire and we have to put it out before the whole city burns down! Now!

So let's get started!!

But how many people will take the time to research solar and wind technologies, investments, public service commissions and utility companies, and food sources—much less look into their own energy habits—then spend an hour or two at a meeting or presentation? All this is a lot to ask; most people simply will not do it. I wouldn't do it unless there were something else there. There has to be something there more than kilowatt-hours and carbon equivalents. The boycott has to have some other dimension…. I'll get into that in a minute.

But first, what about those few people who *would* do the research and come to the meetings? They are important. They are the few who will figure things out for the many. When the panic comes—when the skies are falling and nobody knows which way to turn—when the transition transitions into revolution—that is when these few people and their successors will prove of critical importance. They will know what to do. They will know how to live without fossil fuel. They will be essential because they learned to live without fossil fuel *before they had to live without fossil fuel.* They will be the few who saw the climate crisis in concrete terms, who saw the reality of abstract thought before it became a physical reality.

> If they are organized in groups, they will lead.
> They will lead those in panic and those in transition.

We can borrow encouragement from the words of Margaret Mead, "Never doubt that a small group of thoughtful, committed, citizens can change the world. Indeed, it is the only thing that ever has."

People in transition may not be organized in groups and may not be in a position to lead. By *in transition*, I mean people who are aware of the climate emergency and have taken steps toward sustainable living. They are doing their part. They conserve electricity and heating fuel, walk or bike to work, drive electric cars, and may have solar panels on their rooftops. They set an example for others, but they can lead only if they are organized. Only if they work in community are they in a position to influence the larger society. People in panic and people in transition need the leadership of people in community.

People in community—people who work in groups to find ways

to not buy carbon fuels—are themselves in various stages of transition to renewable energy. Many will have solar and others would have solar if their houses were better suited for it. Hopefully, they will insist on community solar as a way of offsetting their electrical use. But the main difference is that people acting in community are not just "doing their part." They put their money where their mouth is in their personal lives, but do not limit action to the individual level. They work with friends and neighbors to transition the entire community off fossil fuel. They find ways to install solar, drive electric cars, and heat homes sustainably on the individual and collective levels. They begin with the principle of not buying any fossil fuel 10, 20, or 30 years from now, and then figure out how best to make the changes—on the individual, community, municipal, state, federal, and global levels. They get as many people as possible to install rooftop solar, get groups together to create community solar, get Public Service Commissions to allow investor-owned solar, get cities to sign renewable power-purchasing contracts, get the country to initiate a carbon tax, and get the world to develop a comprehensive climate moderation plan.

But where to start?

Find community at church, in the book club, with the neighborhood association, online, in the environmental group, and over the backyard fence. Seek out like-minded people who share your concerns, or maybe you know them already. Form a new group, or form a new interest within an existing group. Go with dues, membership lists, programs, and regular meetings, if that's what feels natural, but avoid unnecessary administrative time and expense. It's easier to work within an existing group, but whatever. It should not cost much, to begin with. It could cost nothing, to begin with. In time, the group may evolve to have more permanent features. You may end up electing a board, hiring staff, choosing an executive director, especially if you are working on the state or municipal level. The original community group may become a subgroup of something larger. But try to keep the community dynamic alive. Try to continue working with friends. Keep a positive peer review dimension to your work. Don't let one personality dominate. Don't let the men dominate. Professional staff can get a lot more work accomplished on the higher levels, but are those people living the vision you are projecting? Is your group still focusing on changing lifestyle choices at the consumer level, or is it becoming just another political pressure group?

What is the demographic of your group? What is its age, class, gender, ethnicity, race, religious, and political composition? Strive for diversity, but not too hard. Be inclusive, but don't worry if you don't have token representatives from every segment of society. It's okay to be mostly middle class, mostly women, mostly white, and mostly Presbyterian or Catholic—just as long as you're aware of potential blind spots in your group's demographic makeup. Know where your particular perspective comes from and welcome diversity to the table when the opportunity arises.

My group, the Renewable Energy Alliance of Louisville, is white, mixed-gender, and middle class. Not surprising. Hopefully our group, and the movement in general, will become more diverse in time, but this is what we have to work with now. We've never had a regular membership roster, never collected dues, and never met regularly except when working on a particular project. We've been together for more than ten years, and some of us longer than that. On the national and global levels we have been affiliated with 350.org. In 2009, we joined Bill McKibben, Wendell Berry, and James Hansen for a civil disobedience event at the coal-burning Capitol Power Plant in Washington. In 2011 we joined a sit-in against the Keystone XL tar sands pipeline at the White House, where many of us were arrested. We're not new to climate issues. But we're getting old, many of us retired or nearing retirement. Some have solar and drive electric cars, but many can't or don't; it's not a requirement. We have time now to do things we could not have earlier in our lives, but we are less flexible—literally and otherwise. It's much harder to make the lifestyle changes we would like to see everywhere around us. Many of us live in older, leafy neighborhoods in older houses with chimneys, dormers, and broken rooflines that do not lend themselves to solar. We are less likely to move to or build a new house. So our main efforts are directed toward community solar, solar legislation in the state legislature, and the 100 percent renewable energy resolution in Louisville. If the Metro Council passes the resolution, we will concentrate on implementation. We may not be around when the last sliver of Arctic sea ice melts in the summer of 2045 or 55, but we hope to see the day when our city shuts down its last coal-fired power plant by 2030, and its last gas-fired plant by 2040.

I hope that the Renewable Energy Alliance of Louisville will concentrate on the carbon boycott in the next few years. I know we're thinking about it. After all these years of driving fossil-fueled cars to protest fossil fuels, we know it's time to get off it ourselves. I'll talk it up, and see what consensus emerges. But I know that, despite our ongoing commitment, it's going to be hard for many of us to make the big changes. Fewer natural opportunities for change, like starting a new job, moving to a new house, an increased salary, or the need for a new car, are on the horizon. We will still try to make changes in our own lives, but may have to settle for inspiring younger folks to choose sustainable jobs, houses, vehicles, commutes, diets, investments, and other lifestyle habits before they get tangled up with big cars and big houses with thermostats. I hope we can inspire younger people to join our group or form their own boycott groups and do things we can only dream of doing at this stage in our lives.

And I hope they are willing to make mistakes. Maybe not the same ones we have made, but mistakes—good ones. This is an evolutionary process. It begins with mutations, and we are the mutations. We don't do things we are expected to do; we don't live the way we are expected to live. We are weird. Much of what we try to do doesn't work. We look silly to those who do what is expected, what is normal. But if you ever want to evolve to a new form, you have to have mutations. You have to have us. You have to have people taking a chance with their lives and their lifestyles—people coloring outside the lines and thinking outside the proverbial box. Young people are good at that. They have the energy to make mistakes. I know: I spent the first part of my life being a young person. I am proud of my mutational heritage and hope to pass that pride on to people in their twenties trying to figure out what kind of living is suitable for the twenty-first century.

I'm weird and I'm proud! Say it loud!

Young people are the stem cells of society. They can develop into a wide range of tissues: ears, noses, hearts, livers, butchers, bakers, and candlestick makers. They can try something for a few years and then turn around and go the other way. They can get a college degree in Eastern Religions and then start a commercial construction company. With a little help from the old folks—or without it—they can begin their working/family lives without fossil fuels and stay off them forever. They will never miss them. They may not need help; they might just need encouragement and the chance to outdo their elders.

A preliminary goal for the carbon boycott could be aiming for a reduction of something like 20 percent. I'm not sure why it works, but I have been told by trusted economists' sources that 20 percent is a magic number. You reduce, increase, or alter a consumer market by that much and it will never be the same again. If you reduce demand for coal- or gas-fired electricity, gasoline, or natural gas by that amount, people will know something is going on. It will be in the newspapers, online, and on television. People will want to know what's behind the big drop, and who is making it happen. Twenty percent (or something like it) will be the tipping point. Before that point, people will wonder what you are doing and why—you will be the mutation. After that point, they will wonder why they are not doing what you are doing. It's called evolution. So get a hold of some consumption figures—state, local, national, global—and set a baseline to see if your community is evolving. Once you get over the 20 percent bump, the rest is downhill. Or so they say.

If 20% doesn't work, try 30%.

Don't stop until 100%.

100% REAL Update: December 5, 2019

The Louisville Committee on Parks and Sustainability discussed the Resolution for 100% Renewable Energy, passed a few minor amendments to it, and then tabled it again. There will be no full council vote on December 12 or for the rest of the year.

Ours is a very individualistic society. We're more proud of our personal achievements than our community achievements. Once we attain a certain level of professional or financial advancement, we're likely to feel ourselves above the crowd. Status is individual and relative. But individualism will not work when everybody—everybody in the world—has to do something together. Being "ahead" of other people in achieving carbon neutrality is as negative as it is positive. Showing off solar panels and fancy electric cars is as likely to alienate as to motivate. Making a big point of recycling rubber bands and used toothpicks can be really obnoxious. Don't be "greener than thou." Your green is meaningless without mine.

The worst form of one-upmanship is calling attention to your environmental effort or idea by badmouthing similar environmental efforts and ideas. Our group has been involved in fighting pipelines on the state, local, national, and even international level. (The KXL crosses the border into Canada.) These are all fossil fuel infrastructure. They promote consumption and long-term dependence on carbon fuels, and they should be stopped before they start. I read online the other day that the movement against fossil fuel pipelines is "unimaginative, short-sighted and simply not true," because pipelines can also be used for hydrogen and renewable methane. OK, that's true, but it won't happen any time soon. Pipelines will be pumping carbon into the atmosphere for decades before they are ever re-purposed for renewable energy. The point here is not that I'm right and the author of the article wrong; the point is that we are working toward the same end and should not be trying to steal attention from one another. I saw another posting on the same site with the title, *Can't Save the Climate by Going Vegan.* I have also seen articles by environmental purists condemning solar panels because they can't be recycled (they can) and even claiming that they absorb heat and make the climate worse. (Really?) When I was fighting the KXL tar sands pipeline some guy wrote in a journal that coal-fired power plants put out more carbon than the pipeline will, so we should fight the power plants and leave the pipeline alone. (Gimme a break!) These authors seem to be saying, "I've figured out something brilliant here—forget everything else." Hey! Cut it out!

From the standpoint of a closed atmosphere, there is no such thing as an individual.

I emphasize this because critics will be ready to pick at what they consider individual violations of their own supposed environmental standard. They will ignore your efforts on the community level, looking instead for individual behavioral shortcomings. "She goes to meetings about carbon emissions, but she drives to the meetings!" Or, "If he hates the gas company so much, why doesn't he cut off the heat to his own house?" During the transitional stage—the next thirty years—the struggle for renewables on the community level will inevitably involve minor hypocrisies on the individual level. You can't build new infrastructure on your way to the meeting. So for now, burn a little gas if you have to. Don't let little stuff get in the way of big stuff. Later, get rid of the fossil car.

Related problems at the organizational stage of a boycott group are *green envy* and *green guilt*. Many people who want to be green can't afford to be. They see others making bold steps into the future but simply cannot do the same things themselves. You want these people in your group. You need them. You want them knocking on doors, making phone calls, writing emails, and organizing events for community solar and a reformed public service commission. They need to know that, at this point in the movement, community work is far more important than individual compliance with unrealizable standards. Make those who may be "out-of-compliance" feel comfortable. Green envy or green guilt is an especially lousy foundation for the creative pursuit of actionable knowledge. Yet I see it regularly. Often, when I mention the possibility of a carbon boycott, I get back a sigh of resignation, or an "I wish I could do that," or a quick defensive run-down of new light bulbs, gas mileage, and attic insulation projects. A lot of people would love to participate in a boycott of all carbon, but think they can't do it. They're right, of course. Nobody can do it now. Nobody can do it alone. It doesn't matter how much carbon you are buying now; in fact, the more you burn now the easier it may be to start using less. The effort is cooperative, not competitive. None of us is carbon neutral until all of us are carbon neutral. Make the change together.

None of us is carbon neutral until all of us are carbon neutral.

That's why we need to organize. The important things now are questions, not answers. How are we going to make this transition? How will we heat our houses thirty years from now? How will we make liquid fuel for airplanes? To become involved in a long-range commitment for answers, all you need are the questions. If you have the answers already, you don't need the group. Welcome people in the group who are just learning about carbon dioxide.

I, for one, do not know how I will visit my children on the other side of the continent without liquid airplane fuel. But I will.

Many buildings we are living in now are not suitable for renewable energy. We need to live with the fossil houses we have now, but stop building new ones! When I was talking about divestment a few chapters back, you may remember that the *Carbon Tracker Initiative* is warning investors away from fossil fuel industries because many of the oil fields, pipelines, and port facilities they are building now cannot possibly live out their useful lives if the world decides to keep global warming below 1.5° or 2° centigrade. The facilities they build now will soon become useless *stranded assets*. The same is true for fossil buildings. If you are living in a leaky old house without good solar exposure, there is a chance it will not make it into the renewable age. It may become stranded. But much worse than living out your remaining years in an old stranded asset is building a new one. Who is going to live in all those huge new mini-mansions sprouting up in the corn-fields? Houses are getting bigger and bigger, and the number of people living in them smaller and smaller. What happens when you can't heat

176

a mini-mansion? I suspect that people building these houses are not aware of what is likely to happen over the next thirty years.

I am worried about privilege: about power and money. Vision proceeds from a social position; people who struggle for their basic needs will not see what I see from here. But I will look. I will look, and build from what I see.

There is a certain privilege in seeing over the landscape. From above the hills, intervening obstacles do not block the view. Vision is broad and far, opening to the horizon. Daily struggles are hidden in low-lying hills and valleys. Work and stress are in the valley, perspective following the terrain. Above the terrain, with a sweep of the eye, there is wholeness; unity becomes truth in practice, love in calculation. Work fulfills vision.

To see the landscape, you need enough. To see the arc of blue, you must stand above the hills and valleys of want and injustice, of wealth and privilege, work and leisure, pain and pleasure, security and risk. You need fun, food, wine, entertainment, friends, family, excitement, stress, and hardship. All good or all bad is not enough. Enough is what you think it is—less than what you think it is. With one robe, what do you lack? Enough is what you need; it is related to wealth but not a function of wealth. To know enough is to open the landscape. In my country, we have too much carbon and not enough. We create privilege in relation to under-privilege, feel guilty, and cannot see. Diversity creates vision but is not enough.

The Ark will be the size of the Earth, built in small places everywhere.

Just above the surface of toil and need, there is wholeness in the relation of humanity to the natural world. Over mountains of strife and injustice, you see the unity of humankind.

The view is essential.

No one has seen it before.

The Carbon Boycott

The climate emergency is the first global crisis. Now is the first time all people are living in the same place. People are the same. We are the same in relation to the atmosphere. Some affect or are affected more than others by air; all live within. Breath folds into the great breath of plants and animals across the oceans and continents. In breath, there is no separation. There are no nations or political parties in the air. We are one. From this height, we are one. It is good to see this, to know it, to breathe it. The privilege to see is good.

Let us build the Ark.
Doing proceeds from seeing.

Community is not the sum of people.
Community is Air breathing among people.

This is the "something more" than kilowatt-hours and carbon equivalents. This is the consciousness that arises from community action that has no enemies. No enemies! How can there be enemies of the same breath? In what way could we not see and do *climate* together? Never before have people had to coordinate action on a global scale. Never. World war? Sure—that was coordination on a global scale. But you need enemies for that. No one has ever had to do anything like this without enemies.

Enemies make it easier. Enemies focus attention.

To be against someone, we draw closer to others against the same someone. Coming together precedes acting together. Action requires agency. There has to be an actor doing the action—a self of some sort—an individual, a state, or an organization. The self has to have a sense of self. The cheapest sense of self is a reflection of non-self—a negative reflection of the enemy.

There is talk of eliminating carbon dioxide, of banning fracking and gasoline engines, but who is going to do it? By what agency do China, Russia, Mozambique, Brazil, and the United States eliminate carbon together? There is no one to be against, no reflection. Who coordinates, cajoles, and enforces? What if some superpower decides to opt out? You can't have that. There has to be a unified mechanism on the global level to plan, activate, and administer an ongoing mandatory program of atmospheric management. This is a danger to national sovereignty. This is a violation of national sovereignty. Our first identity is with the nation. Practical response to the climate crisis violates the paradigm of national sovereignty.

Division or unity will be a choice.

That is why we go to boring meetings about kilowatt-hours and carbon dioxide equivalents. We want the world to live on. It's not about solar panels and municipal power purchasing plans; it's about the human spirit. We are going to need some. It begins when two or three are gathered together. That is the grassroots level. The higher up you go the more paradigm you take with you.

United, there is no need for tools to destroy ourselves.

100 % REAL Update: December 14, 2019

I hiked today with twenty-four concerned citizens, REAL members and friends, through the section of Bernheim Forest where Louisville Gas and Electric plans to build a natural gas pipeline. The proposed easement is about a mile long, crossing two hills and a small stream in the valley below. As I stood on a slope overlooking the woods and sedge fields, I saw battle lines forming: trees, birds, snails, squirrels, bobcats, and wildflowers facing off against chain saws, backhoes, and bulldozers. We didn't have a chance. Behind their lines was an army of lawyers, legislators, and a bulging, inchoate demand for more houses, factories, jobs, and money.

There were faces but I did not see who they were. They needed this. They would never see it, but they needed this place. They did not know they were here. Behind where I stood, men and women were gathering, some shouting, fists raised in the air, others staring across the land without expression, wondering if there would be lathis.

No.

But here, on this hillside where the Air is thick, there will be a price.

For now, the courts will decide.

100% REAL Update: January 15, 2020

Still no vote on the 100% Renewable Energy Resolution. The chairwoman of the Parks and Sustainability Committee of the Louisville Metro Council tells me that the resolution needs a "financial impact" statement, though it includes no specific implementations and therefore has no specific financial impact. The delay may be push back from other interested parties. The measure will die if there is no vote next month, and a vote seems unlikely with this sort of delay.

We will reintroduce it immediately.

Meanwhile, 100% REAL is growing in numbers and local support. We are covered by local media, interviewed on local radio programs, and invited to speak to local groups. We are onto a Truth.

100% REAL Update: February 5, 2020

On short notice, the Parks and Sustainability Committee held a special meeting this afternoon to consider the Resolution for 100% Renewable Energy. We were surprised. About 20 100% REAL members scrambled to attend the meeting. The resolution passed by a 4 to 2 vote, with one abstention, and was added to the agenda for tomorrow's meeting of the full Metro Council.

100% REAL Update: February 6, 2020

Twenty-five members of 100% REAL showed up in front of City Hall before the council meeting for a short, low-volume demonstration. Others arrived inside for the meeting itself. Two of us spoke before the Council in support of the Resolution. The resolution sponsor and the committee chairwoman urged passage. Debate ensued. Several opponents thought it would be too expensive and did not want to force individuals to conserve, recycle, or use renewable energy. Other council members spoke with passionate concern for the well-being of future generations. Opponents came back with the "financial impact" issue. Fears mounted of further objections, delays, and yet another tabling of the measure. The evening wore on. Just before 9 p.m., a vote was called and seconded: 15 in favor, 4 opposed, 7 did not vote. Despite the late hour, the mayor (who was not at the meeting) immediately issued a statement supporting 100% renewable energy for the city, including a plan for a citywide energy audit and a professional energy manager. We went out for a hard-won beer.

Now, all we have to do is do it.

There is no end; there are only means.

*   *   *

An Arc of Blue rises above the mountain slopes of strife, ignorance, and war, promising a new covenant. A narrow curvature of Air covers Earth and Sea.

An Ark floats over the rising deep.

Air is unity; the gravitational force of air keeps plants and people on the land, growing toward the Sun.

Bibliography

Barber, James. *Mandela's World: The International Dimension of South Africa's Political Revolution 1990–99*. Athens: Ohio University Press, 2004.

Brown, Judith M., and Anthony Parel, eds. *The Cambridge Companion to Gandhi*. New York: Cambridge University Press, 2011.

Carp, Benjamin L. *Defiance of the Patriots: The Boston Tea Party & the Making of America*. New Haven: Yale University Press, 2010.

Counts, Cecelie. "Divestment Was Just One Weapon in Battle Against Apartheid," *New York Times*, updated January 27, 2013.

Dubow, Saul. *Apartheid 1948–1994*. Oxford: Oxford University Press, 2014.

Elton, Sarah. *Consumed: Food for a Finite Planet*. New York: HarperCollins Publishers Limited, 2013.

Garrow, David J. *The Walking City: The Montgomery Bus Boycott, 1955–56*. Brooklyn, NY: Carlson, 1989.

Global Nonviolent Action Database, Swarthmore College. https://nvdatabase. swarthmore.edu/category/wave-campaigns/south-africa-apartheid-divestment-movement-1970s-1980s.

Guha, Ramachandra. *Gandhi: The Years that Changed the World, 1914–1948*. New York: Knopf, 2018.

Hare, Kenneth. *They Walked to Freedom: The Story of the Montgomery Bus Boycott*. Champaign, IL: Spotlight Press, 2005.

Lansing, Paul. "The Divestment of United States Companies in South Africa and Apartheid." *Nebraska Law Review*. Volume 60, Issue 2, Article 4, 1981.

Lappé, Anna. *Diet for a Hot Planet: The Climate Crisis at the End of Your Fork and What You Can Do About It*. New York: Bloomsbury, 2010.

Lappé, Francis Moore. *Diet for a Small Planet*. New York: Balantine Books, 1971.

Little, Amanda. *The Fate of Food: What We'll Eat in a Bigger, Hotter, Smarter World*. New York: Harmony Books, 2019.

Mihaly, Christy, and Sue Heavenrich. *Diet for a Changing Climate: Food for Thought*. Minneapolis: Twenty-First Century Books, 2019.

Palmer, Lisa. *Hot, Hungry Planet: The Fight to Stop a Global Food Crisis in the Face of Climate Change*. New York: St. Martin's Press, 2017.

Redmond, John C. *Three to Ride*. New York: Hamilton Books, 2012.

Ruhe, Peter. *Gandhi*. New York: Phaidon Press, 2001.

Shaarma, Arvind. *Gandhi: A Spiritual Biography*. New Haven: Yale University Press, 2013.

Slaughter, Thomas P. *Independence: The Tangled Roots of the American Revolution.* New York: Hill and Wang, 2014.

Thompson, Leonard. *A History of South Africa.* New Haven: Yale University Press, 2001.

Unger, Harlow Giles. *American Tempest: How the Boston Tea Party Sparked a Revolution.* Philadelphia: Da Capo Press, 2011.

Volo, James M. *The Boston Tea Party: The Foundations of Revolution.* Santa Barbara, CA: Praeger, 2012.

Weber, Thomas. "Gandhian Nonviolence and the Salt March." *Social Alternatives,* Vol. 21, no.2, Autumn, 2002.

Welsh, David. *The Rise and Fall of Apartheid.* Charlottesville: University of Virginia Press, 2009.

Wolpert, Stanley. *Gandhi's Passion: The Life and Legacy of Mahatma Gandhi.* New York: Oxford University Press, 2001.

Index